The Ten Commandments of Christian Parenting

A Common Sense Guide for

Raising Children in a Technically

Advanced Society

By David E. Miller, Ph.D.

Psychologist

LONGWOOD
COMMUNICATIONS

To contact the author, write: Published by:
David E. Miller, PhD   Longwood Communications
7664 Slate Ridge Boulevard   397 Kingslake Drive
Reynoldsburg, OH 43068-3126   DeBary, FL 32713
                                       904-774-1991

Dedication

This book is dedicated to several people who played significant parts in motivating me to write it. Among them are the many Christian parents who have worked with me in family therapy, sincerely searching for answers and demonstrating the need for such project. Our own two children, Scott and Lori, developed into beautiful Christian young persons, despite the mistakes we made as parents. Their acceptance and now endorsement of the values my wife and I taught have confirmed and inspired this writing. Many thanks are also due our own godly parents, who have encouraged me in my practice and supported it as a ministry to God's people. Finally, this book is dedicated to future generations of parents who will search for ways to raise their children in Christian homes while living in a wordly society that minimizes traditional values.

Contents

Prologue

Is Christian Parenting Possible?

Show me your ways, O Lord, teach me your paths;
guide me in your truth and teach me, for you are
God my savior, and my hope is in you all day long.
Psalm 25: 4-5

In today's fast-paced world, many Christian parents ask whether there is sufficient time to do an adequate job of raising their children. Within the Christian home, parenting responsibilities should rank extremely high among other tasks and be considered an important obligation, a privilege, and a great opportunity to raise children in the sight of God. However, many parents struggle to manage their time and priorities in ways that minimize adverse effects on child rearing. Others feel guilty for not having spent enough time on parenting.

Even if we temporarily disregard the extra effort

required of *Christian* parents, parenting is one of the most difficult roles in adult life. It is both time-consuming and exhausting, constantly draining available energy levels despite its rewards. At times, parents may feel their parenting tasks are thankless, having few benefits or rewards. At other times, perhaps too infrequently, parents receive a glimmer of appreciation for all the hard work exerted on behalf of their children.

Parenting quite often becomes secondary to other things that demand one's full attention, such as earning a livelihood. In addition to the 40 to 50 hours weekly that most jobs require, there are overtime hours that one is expected to share with co-workers and spend on extra projects, committee meetings, and planning seminars or conferences. Such activities are necessary to advancing in a career and all seem legitimate, yet these obligations compete for a parent's limited time and energy.

Aside from work commitments, school, community, and church involvement as well as other activities take their toll on parents. Organizing child care, making preschool arrangements, attending parent-teacher conferences, supporting little league sports and music lessons, and other extracurricular activities important to children's development are only a few of the tasks facing most parents today. Life becomes even more complicated when one spouse is completing college-level courses or some other form of advanced training that is necessary to retain a job or advance in a career.

A vicious cycle develops as parents find themselves with less-than-adequate time and energy to handle the tasks needing their attention. Despite appropriate priorities, the fast pace we maintain and the demanding society in which we live do not allow sufficient time for everything. Also, many people lack the skills to organize and manage their time effectively, resulting in inefficient use of already limited time.

Quite often, friends request Christians' assistance or ask them to lend a supporting hand. Christians are supposed to be helpful to others — that's what we've learned from early childhood. Although we feel stressed and stretched to the maximum, we find it difficult to explain this concern to others. Quite often we respond to their requests for help although we do not have time to add even one more thing to an already busy schedule. Unfortunately, family or parenting commitments are quite often postponed. It somehow seems easier to explain to the ones we love the most (family) rather than social acquaintances our inability to keep a commitment. It seems that our family members should understand how busy we are and more willingly accept our inability to give them time.

Quite often a request for help may be made by a pastor or another church leader who we feel is God's servant. A pastor's urgent plea may be made in a manner which conveys that we are uniquely talented and have the necessary attributes for the task at hand. It is further reasoned that there is just no one else who can be recruited, for everyone knows there are few willing workers in most congregations. Perhaps that is why many pastors, in desperation, allow themselves to place many more responsibilities with certain people than they are able to balance with family priorities. With continual urging, a parent's position on priorities may weaken, and perhaps before giving further thought or prayer to the matter, a requested task is reluctantly accepted. In this decision-making process, the issues with the most pressure attached seem to rank higher; the old "squeaky wheel gets the grease" phenomenon seems to apply.

Scripture instructs Christians to seek first God's kingdom and His righteousness, and all these things will be given to them (see Matthew 6:33). Some Christians and even perhaps some well-meaning pastors misinterpret this scripture to mean "putting God *and church* first" rather than "God first" as intended. God does not and never has intended for anyone to put even the church before family. I Timothy 3:5 states, "If anyone does not know how to manage his own family, how can he take care of God's church?" This implies that people can serve God yet lose their families, and that perhaps God's expectation for the Christian is to rank family as a prerequisite for church work, so that a more balanced commitment can be made.

Some parents so diligently serve their church in a multitude of roles that they become exhausted and cannot deal with their family. This over-involvement can be an escape from parental or marital obligations — perhaps even a shirking of responsibility. Over-involvement precludes the ability to deal effectively with one's marriage and family. A large number of Christian families suddenly find themselves in the middle of marital dysfunction, family conflicts, difficulties in parent-child relationships and communication, and a host of other problems that necessitate professional services from a counselor or psychologist.

Obviously, some will go to the other extreme and

use the need for family time as an excuse to be totally uninvolved and detached. This extreme is just as wrong! One must take a balanced approach to time commitments, making time for the essentials. People usually do what they really want to do, and if the church is prioritized as an essential, it will be given a high priority but not at the expense of family.

It is not my purpose to cause parents to feel worse than they already may regarding their parental roles or to place them on guilt trips. Even though modern society has contributed heavily to the time-commitment dilemma, the issue has been raised throughout history. Philosophers have referred to this problem as early as in Socrates' time, as illustrated by the following excerpt from one of his early writings:

> If I could climb the highest place in Athens, I would lift my voice and proclaim…Fellow citizens, why do ye turn and scrape every stone to gather wealth, and take so little care of your children to whom one day you must relinquish it all?

The Christian parent must seek insight from Scripture. In Matthew 18, Jesus refers to children as greatest in the kingdom of heaven (see vs. 1-4). The chapter relates the occasion when Jesus' disciples came to Him, asking which one of them would be the greatest in His kingdom. Not only did Jesus answer their question, but He demonstrated through his analogy that children are very important creatures, not to be minimized, ignored, or forgotten. Rather than present adults as models for children, Christ stated that adults should take notice of and model themselves after children. He went on to demonstrate His feelings regarding children by saying "And whoever welcomes a little child like this is my name welcomes me" (see vs. 5). This exhortation of Christ to His disciples further warns that it would be better for a man to have a large millstone tied around his neck and be drowned in a deep sea as to being found guilty of misleading a child (see vs. 6). This analogy very concisely demonstrates the importance of children and the responsibility that parents have toward them.

Another important implication is found in Matthew 6:33, which reads, "But seek first His Kingdom and His righteousness, and all these things will be given to you as well." In Matthew 6:34, parents are reminded not to worry about tomorrow since tomorrow will worry about itself, and there being enough trouble in a day that one should not give rise to additional ones. So often, we worry about the implications of our time constraints but do little to change our patterns of behavior. This scripture exhorts Christians to place their many tasks and limited time in God's hands and ask for help to order them accordingly. We must look carefully at our priorities and perhaps eliminate some otherwise worthy activities that deprive our children of the loving companionship that is so essential to their growth. In John 15:5, we are reminded that even if our priorities are worked out in our minds, we still need God. It is only through Him that we can be fruitful in our endeavors. "I am the vine; you are the branches. If a man remains in me and I in him, he will bear much fruit; apart from me you can do nothing."

Not only is Christian parenting a value upheld by Scripture, but to fail in this very important calling has some serious ramifications. First of all, most parents recognize very early that they have become their child's most significant people or "super heroes." Parents rank alongside the most favorite cartoon or storybook characters. This is one of the reasons parents enjoy their little tikes so much. Affirmation from young children gives many rewards and much satisfaction to parents despite the other challenges and responsibilities that characterize the parenting role. Although parents recognize that they don't have all the answers and are not the smartest or strongest people in the world, they enjoy being made to feel that way by a son's or daughter's early belief system. Parents, therefore, have a very important responsibility — to provide gentle guidance to young lives and minds. Because parents have a very significant influence in a child's development, they must be conscientious in living out their parental roles.

One very important theory supported by a large number of psychologists and child development specialists indicates that children learn about others by first learning about their family and home environment; they then apply this knowledge to others. The following poem by Dorothy Law Nolte, often displayed in the offices of child psychologists and other child development specialists, probably summarizes this theory best:

Children Learn What They Live

If a child lives with criticism, he learns to condemn.
If a child lives with hostility, he learns to fight.
If a child lives with ridicule, he learns to be shy.
If a child lives with shame, he learns to feel guilty.
If a child lives with tolerance, he learns to be patient.
If a child lives with encouragement, he learns
    confidence.
If a child lives with praise, he learns to appreciate.
If a child lives with security, he learns to have faith.
If a child lives with approval, he learns to like himself.
If a child lives with acceptance and friends, he learns to
    find love in the world.

If children learn from the behavior observed within their own families how to respond to other people, they must also, perhaps much more importantly, develop an image of God through their image of their parents. This elevates the importance of Christian parenting. If a child perceives his parents as unforgiving, he then perceives God as unforgiving. Critical or intolerant parents will no doubt cause their children to attribute similar qualities to God. On the other hand, parents who convey approval, acceptance, security, and fairness contribute positively to their child's developing concept and understanding of God. For this reason, it is most important that parents take a serious look at the attributes they are teaching their children through modeling.

Some Christians have a perception that since they are Christians they need not worry about the problems commonly associated with inadequate parenting. This is a false assumption and a dangerous oversimplification of God's protection of His children. An increasing number of Christian families are finding themselves in situations requiring professional services. In modern-day society many forces impact our children's lives in addition to parenting efforts. This is precisely why parenting must be a high priority. Parents compete with some rather powerful influences — television, peers, school, neighborhood, changing values, the moral decay of society — which together monopolize more of a child's time than parental influence and guidance.

Don't become overwhelmed or give up from discouragement! Although Christian parenting has always been a challenge and will remain so for years to come, *it is possible to successfully meet this challenge!*

I

ESTABLISHING A GOOD PARENT-CHILD RELATIONSHIP

Be imitators of God, therefore, as dearly loved
children and live a life of love, just as Christ loved
us and gave himself up for us as a fragrant offering
and sacrifice to God.
Ephesians 5:1

Parents are not automatically ordained with authority when they become parents. They must establish a relationship with their children and become "significant others," persons whom they love and respect. William Dahms describes authority as a relationship issue.[1] Simply stated, one has no authority over a child unless there is some relationship between that person and the child. As the relationship grows, the level of authority increases.

A *quality relationship* is one in which the child feels that those in authority are caring, honest, fair, right, reasonable, dependable, and openly supportive and respectful.[2] Although Dahms refers mainly of staff members and teachers in schools or other children's programs, much of what he writes is completely relevant regarding parents and the relationship they have with their children.

Many parents practice methods precisely opposite of what Dr. Dahms advocates for a healthy parent-child relationship. When the relationship is lacking, the adult often resorts to intimidation, threats, fear, and other unhealthy approaches of control. Such methods usually are ineffective in changing a child's behavior. If changes do occur, they are usually superficial and short-lived. How many times have you heard parents say to their children, "You'll do it because I say so," "You'll do it or else," "Don't you dare talk to me like that. I'm your father"? In my work with parents, I often share a story of a little boy whose mother asked him to be seated, without success. After the boy adamantly refused several times, his mother forcibly sat him in a chair and held him there. Even though she had gained physical control of his body, the little boy looked at his mother obstinately and said, "I may be sitting on the outside, but I'm standing on the inside!" We are not always winning the battle, even when it appears we are.

How, then, are parents supposed to gain a quality relationship with their children? Our earlier definition of a quality relationship implies that the caregiver or parent be seen as caring, honest, fair, right, reasonable, dependable, and openly supportive and respectful. Parents must behave in a manner that demonstrates these positive qualities to build such a good relationship with their children.

In examining these qualities further, let's first look

at *caring,* which can be demonstrated in a multitude of ways at all age levels. When a child is an infant, parents must care for every aspect of the child's life, from feeding to changing dirty diapers. Adolescents no longer need or want such assistance but need to know that parents support and love them, and that they will be available if necessary. The manner in which the parent accomplishes this will convey to children the level of care available to them.

We can also communicate care by the way we talk to our children. A caring exchange conveys respect. Adults don't have to talk down to a child or be condescending. The overall manner of handling children's needs will convey how precious a commodity they are. Some children quickly perceive how carelessly they are handled by parents or other adults who at the same time seem to give the utmost care to a piece of antique furniture, an automobile, or something else of value. The value we as parents place on our parenting responsibilities is revealed by how we care for our children. Involvement in children's lives is a good indication of parental care. From showing interest in homework to playing house, from attending little league games to loaning the family car for that important date — these are all ways to convey interest in their lives and the importance we place on their comfort and happiness.

Honesty is necessary for a positive relationship. We should never hide the truth from our children. We can explain things to them much better than any other source they might eventually seek out for responses to unanswered questions. If something is hidden from children to protect them, they will quite often need

17

explanations at a later time. When things are clarified later, you may also need to handle why the truth was hidden or kept secret to begin with, which may make children feel distrusted or unimportant. Children tend to work out their own rationale regarding family problems or perceived difficulties if explanations are not provided by their parents. Many children perceive marital difficulty within their family before their parents proactively deal with it, often blaming themselves or their behavior for mom and dad's unhappiness. Minor problems may be misinterpreted by children as serious threats to their family and cause feelings of insecurity and anxiety. Children are too perceptive for parents to hide family secrets from them. Of course, one must use common sense and recognize the developmental level of the child in determining to what extent details should be shared. But family secrets are never right!

Fairness is a prerequisite for establishing a positive parent-child relationship. It is sometimes hard for parents to be fair since many perceive themselves as having or needing to have ultimate power over their children. Listening to a child's explanation for misbehavior and giving explanations for discipline is a step in the right direction. Caution should be used in stating to a child that he or she must follow the same rules as a brother or sister; because every child is unique, each may require a different approach to discipline. Rules need to be flexible to accommodate a variety of situations; parents should try to avoid being too rigid with their children. For example, curfews and responsibilities need to be age-appropriate. Obviously, a teenager demonstrating more trustworthy behavior may be legitimately rewarded with fewer boundaries than one who constantly pushes limits and exhibits irresponsible behaviors. A more rigid structure is required for children experiencing school problems to facilitate completion of homework and tutoring.

In some families, parents need to help their children understand financial matters and the need to equitably distribute limited family resources to meet all members' needs. Parents should be careful to prevent younger children from always getting what is left over — either material goods such as hand-me-down clothing or what is left over of the parents' time. A plan that works for many families is scheduling individual time for each child, along with time for activities that include everyone.

Parents should strive to *be right* and have the credibility and respect that one acquires for being right. Although we must remain open to admitting when we are wrong, we should strive to model correct behaviors and attitudes. As our children get older, they recognize our limitations and inform us of our inconsistencies. Parents must not panic or reject such feedback, for this is very normal as a child matures. Children simply recognize their parents' limitations as they strive to develop their own competencies as individuals.

Perhaps the best way to reveal the perception that one is right is to live rightly. The most powerful way to communicate our sense of right and wrong is by how we live.[3] As already described, honesty and caring go a long way toward conveying fairness. Obviously, being reasonable in the expectations we place on our children as well as being willing to listen to their concerns will help them see we are attempting to be fair. We should avoid preaching honesty to our children if we model dishonesty by cheating on our income tax or driving away from a parked car we have just backed into without notifying the owner. Our actions speak louder than words in situations like these; such actions teach children our true values and morals.

Being reasonable is much like being fair. The best method to demonstrate this quality is to eliminate any perception of its opposite — rigidity. Rules, regulations, requests, or instructions are not reasonable just because parents have made them. We should try to avoid explaining a rule by the explanation "because I say so." Children deserve to have explanations. Without getting into answering every "why" raised by our children, we should try to explain the rationale for our decisions or discipline. This process needs to be educational as it will help them understand and learn values. Although this process takes time and effort, it may assist them in becoming good parents to our grandchildren.

The next important means of building a relationship with one's child is to *be dependable*. Dependability goes further than just providing for their needs consistently. Parents need to prioritize spending quality time with their children and be conscientious in fulfilling this commitment. If our children can't depend on us, who can they depend on? We should never make promises we can't keep — this only weakens the child's view of our dependability. As dependable parents, we need to be seen as people who can predict when our child will need help and offer our support. The most dependable people I know are my best friends. Perhaps being your child's best friend will ensure this quality of dependability.

Being supportive and respectful starts within the home and is then applied to the extended family and other people. Children learn to respect their parents because they respect each other. Children also learn to trust parents because they demonstrate trust with others. Parents should look for opportunities to convey respect and support as well as model their support for each other. Comments such as "Let's see how your dad feels about this" or "Let's discuss it with your mother" reinforce this quality. Of course, we must be genuine in our efforts. It is very difficult to fool our children; they perceive our attitudes and motives despite our attempts to hide them.

Several years ago while attending an open house at our daughter's school, I received a handout entitled *"Five Ingredients for Effective Parenting."* These ingredients are closely related to building an appropriate parent-child relationship:

1. *Demonstrate mutual respect.*
   Limit yelling, lecturing, hitting, sarcasm, doing things for children they can do for themselves, double standards, and negative talk.

2. *Take time for fun.*
   The quantity of time is less important than quality of time; spend time each day on things both you and your children can enjoy doing.

3. *Use encouragement.*
   Avoid praising the *child* — praise his or her *efforts*, for such tends to build a sense of adequacy.

21

4. *Communicate love.*
   This should be done through verbal and nonverbal means.

5. *Listen to what the child is not saying.*
   Tune in to the message behind the signal.

Another important issue very closely associated to the parent-child relationship is the parents' attitude. In the Prologue, we tried to illustrate the privilege God has given us as parents. We have also emphasized that the parenting process takes much time and energy if we are going to go about it successfully. The attitude of the parent has a lot to do with how much "work" it becomes. A concept I frequently reference in my work with parents is that *problems are opportunities.* Any time a behavior problem occurs a parent should be semi-enthusiastic, since it becomes an opportunity — both for the parent to teach a value and for the child to learn that value. Such a situation is usually a good learning experience since it springs from real life. Of course, "semi-enthusiasm" does not mean that as Dad catches a lamp that has been overturned in a fight between his children that he leaps for joy and exclaims, "Oh, just what I've been waiting for all day! Another opportunity to teach my children proper social skills!" Obviously not! He frantically jumps in to break up the fight and tries to save the lamp in the process. His response is probably more human than described above, and he might even be a little angry at his undersocialized offspring, who surely take after their mother's side of the family.

If parents can approach a problem with a positive attitude, they can minimize negative effects and reach a solution more easily. Problems are a normal part of life. Edmund Cooke once said, "Trouble is what you make it." Depending upon what we make it, a problem can be devastating or growth enhancing. There is little we can do to prevent some problems from occurring. It is our attitude that allows a problem to remain a problem or makes it an opportunity for growth. We must approach problems in a proactive rather than reactive manner. Adopting a calm attitude helps to restore calm. This also reduces any tendency to react negatively and damage the relationships that we are working to develop and maintain.

Parents do need to convey optimism in their parenting efforts. If parents try to increase their understanding of their child's behavior, carefully listen to what their children say through words and actions, and concentrate on building a positive parent-child relationship, they will increase their chances for successfully maintaining a positive attitude. Perhaps the most important way to maintain a positive approach with children is to believe in them as individuals. I believe all kids are born to win! Unfortunately, many of them have been conditioned to lose.[4] This conditioning process begins and ends with a child doubting himself or herself, which is usually the result of careless interactions with the significant adults in that child's life.

II

Developing Good Communication

Do not let any unwholesome talk come out of your mouths, but only what is helpful for building others up according to their needs, that it may benefit those who listen.
Ephesians 4:29

Thousands of articles, papers, and books have been written on the subject of communication. The manner in which we communicate determines to a large extent just how effective we are at problem solving. When communication channels break down, problem-solving efforts usually cease. This is true with all kinds of interpersonal interaction, including communication between spouses within a marriage, employer-employee relations, management-union negotiations, and parent-child relationships. We will focus on communication between parent and child, identify styles of interaction that are more effective in solving problems, and target stumbling blocks to effective communication and problem solving.

In *Parent Effectiveness Training*, Thomas Gordon refers to twelve ways in which people communicate a majority of the time. Some of these are not only ineffective but cause further problems for both the person sending the message and the listener, who may hear a distorted message. Others are less problematic; however, *none of these twelve methods should become the predominant mode for parent-child communications.* A summary of these methods with examples of each follow:[5]

1. *Ordering, Directing, Commanding*
   Telling the child to do something; giving an order or a command:
   "I don't care what other parents say; you have to do the yard work!"
   "Don't talk to your mother like that!"
   "Now you go back up there and play with Ginny and Joyce!"
   "Stop complaining!"

2. *Warning, Admonishing, Threatening*
   Telling the child what consequences will occur if he or she does something:
   "If you do that, you'll be sorry!"
   "One more statement like that and you'll leave the room!"
   "You'd better not do that if you know what's good for you!"

3. *Exhorting, Moralizing, Preaching*

Telling the child what he or she ought to do:
"You shouldn't act like that."
"You ought to…"
"You must always respect your elders."

4. *Advising, Giving Solutions or Suggestions*
   Telling the child how to solve a problem, giving advice or suggestions; providing answers or solutions:
   "Why don't you ask both Ginny and Joyce to play down here?"
   "Just wait a couple of years before deciding on college."
   "I suggest you talk to your teachers about that."
   "Go make friends with some other girls."

5. *Lecturing, Teaching, Giving Logical Arguments*
   Trying to influence the child with facts, counterarguments, logic, information, or your own opinions:
   "College can be the most wonderful experience you'll ever have."
   "Children must learn how to get along with each other."
   "Let's look at the facts about college graduates."
   "If kids learn to take responsibility around the house, they'll grow up to be responsible adults."
   "Look at it this way — your mother needs help around the house."
   "When I was your age, I had twice as much to do as you."

6. *Judging, Criticizing, Disagreeing, Blaming*
   Making a negative judgment or evaluation of the child:
   "You're not thinking clearly."
   "That's an immature point of view."
   "You're very wrong about that."
   "I couldn't disagree with you more."

7. *Praising, Agreeing*
   Offering a positive evaluation or judgment, agreeing:
   "Well, I think you're pretty."
   "You have the ability to do well."
   "I think you're right."
   "I agree with you."

8. *Name-Calling, Ridiculing, Shaming*
   Making the child feel foolish, putting the child into a category, shaming him or her:
   "You're a spoiled brat."
   "Look here, Mr. Smarty..."
   "You're acting like a wild animal."
   "Okay, little baby."

9. *Interpreting, Analyzing, Diagnosing*
   Telling children what their motives are or analyzing why they are doing or saying something; communicating that you have them figured out or diagnosed:
   "You're just jealous of Ginny."
   "You're saying that to bug me."
   "You really don't believe that at all."

"You feel that way because you're not doing well in school."

10. *Reassuring, Sympathizing, Consoling, Supporting*

Trying to make the child feel better, talking him out of his feelings, trying to make his feelings go away, denying the strength of his feelings:

"You'll feel different tomorrow."

"All kids go through this sometime."

"Don't worry; things'll work out."

"You could be an excellent student, with your potential."

"I used to think that too."

"I know; school can be pretty boring sometimes."

"You usually get along with other kids very well."

11. *Probing, Questioning, Interrogating*

Trying to find reasons, motives, causes; searching for more information to help you solve the problem:

"When did you start feeling this way?"

"Why do you suppose you hate school?"

"Do the kids ever tell you why they don't want to play with you?"

"How many other kids have you talked to about the work they have to do?"

"Who put that idea into your head?"

"What will you do if you don't go to college?"

12. Withdrawing, Distracting, Humoring, Diverting

Trying to get the child away from the problem; withdrawing from the problem yourself; distracting the child, kidding him out of it, pushing the problem aside:

"Just forget about it."

"Let's not talk about it at the table."

"Come on — let's talk about something more pleasant."

"How's it going with your basketball?"

"Why don't you try burning the school building down?"

"We've been through all this before."

Although many of the above examples can be effective communication tools at times, Gordon refers to them as "the typical twelve," quite often leading to ineffective communication. This is not to imply they are always bad or never to be used, for there are times that "questioning" to gain further information or "sympathizing" with someone might indeed be helpful. "Praising" can be an excellent tool to use with children, for it greatly facilitates building self-esteem. However, if the predominant style of communicating takes on these forms to the exclusion of listening, one can expect to be misunderstood much of the time.

A good number of parents use ordering, preaching, advising, and judging predominantly. However, if they are asked about why they are so negative with their children, they will deny utilizing those styles and rename their communication by such names as "teaching," "advising," and "interpreting" since these latter styles represent qualities of good parenting. No one would question that a good parent teaches, advises, and interprets for their children.

If this is the case, why then are these methods considered inadequate parent to child communication techniques? Dr. Gordon indicates that about 99 out of 100 parents participating in Parent Effectiveness Training classes use ineffective methods of communication with their children. What most parents say to children usually does nothing to resolve the problem and instead may worsen the conflict or disagreement. While some interactions cause a child to resist a parent's influence by refusing to change his or her behavior, other interactions make the child feel dumb and insulted. Still other interactions make children feel guilty, tear down self-esteem, and cause them to defend themselves vigorously or provoke them to attack parents in a "get-you-back" fashion.[6] Some of us make the mistake of sending a "solution message" to the child; we convey to them what we feel they should do. As parents, we take over by calling the shots and maintaining control. We do this by utilizing one of the four styles described below:[7]

1. *ORDERING, DIRECTING, COMMANDING*
   "You go find something to play with."
   "Stop wrinkling the paper."
   "Put those pots and pans away."
   "You clean up that mess."

2. *WARNING, ADMONISHING, THREATENING*
   "If you don't stop, I'll scream."
   "Mother will get angry if you don't get out from under my feet."
   "If you don't get out there and put that kitchen back the way it was, you're going to be sorry."

3. *EXHORTING, PREACHING, MORALIZING*
   "Don't ever interrupt a person when he's reading."
   "Please play someplace else."
   "You shouldn't play when Mother is in a hurry."
   "Always clean up after yourself."

4. *ADVISING, GIVING, SUGGESTIONS OR SOLUTIONS*
   "Why don't you go outside and play?"
   "Let me suggest something else for you to do."
   "Can't you put each thing away after you use it?"

Parents would never talk to another adult the way they quite often talk to their children. For example, if a friend comes over to our home and happens to place his foot on the rung of our new dining room chair, we would never say what most of us say to our children:[8]

"Get your feet off my chair this minute."

"You should never put your feet on somebody's new chair."

"If you know what's good for you, you'll take your feet off my chair."

"I suggest you do not ever put your feet on my
    chair."

While some of us send solution messages, others of us send "put-down messages." Everyone knows the discomfort that comes after having received a put-down message. Such messages convey blame, judgment, ridicule, criticism, or shame. According to Gordon , put-down messages fall into one of the following categories:[9]

1. JUDGING, CRITICIZING, BLAMING
    "You ought to know better."
    "You are being very thoughtless."
    "You are being naughty."
    "You are the most inconsiderate child I know."
    "You'll be the death of me yet."

2. Name-Calling, Ridiculing, Shaming
    "You're a spoiled brat."
    "All right, Mister Busybody…"
    "Do you like being a selfish freeloader?"
    "Shame on you."

3. Interpreting, Diagnosing, Psychoanalyzing
    "You just want to get some attention."
    "You're trying to get my goat."
    "You just love to see how far you can go before
      I get mad."
    "You always want to play just where I'm
      working."

Developing Good Communication

4. Teaching, Instructing
"It's not good manners to interrupt someone."
"Nice children don't do that."
"How would you like it if I did that to you?"
"Why don't you be good for a change?"
"Do unto others…"
"We don't leave our dishes dirty."

All of these put-downs, which depreciate the child as a person and attack his or her self-esteem, cause feelings of inadequacy and resistance on the child's part. These responses are defenses chosen by children to deal with these unfair interactions from their parents, whom they can't help but feel are unfair. "These are the ways that parents, day after day, contribute to the destruction of their children's ego or self-esteem. Like drops of water falling on a rock, these daily messages gradually, imperceptibly leave a destructive effect on children."[10]

As already indicated above, there are probably times when each one of the styles making up this list can be very appropriate and necessary. However, each style of communication in this list is potentially hazardous if used out of the appropriate context. Potential misunderstanding or misperception is increased when we adopt these forms as predominant styles.

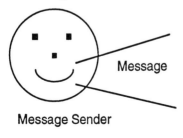

Message

Message Sender

Message Receiver

Communication is a two-way street. Any interaction includes the *sender* and the *receiver.*

Sometimes a receiver only takes in what he or she would like to hear. This phenomenon is referred to as "tunnel hearing."

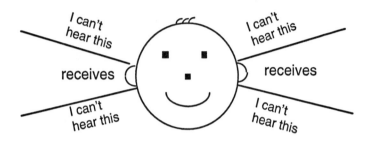

Tunnel hearing prevents us from really listening to others. Many parents are guilty of tunnel or selective hearing when it comes to their children. Children quickly learn the science of tunnel hearing through adult modeling. Some children look at their parents with deep concentration and still do not hear the truths imparted. Although the message may have been clearly and concisely delivered, leaving no doubt in the parent's mind as to its meaning, that message wasn't received as intended. If a transmission hasn't been properly received, then there has not been communication.

Consider a boy coming home after school. As he comes through the door he says, "Hi Mom, what's for dinner?" His mother knows that he has probably not taken a sudden interest in nutrition or the evening menu, so long as it excludes such things as asparagus, broccoli, green beans, and peas. His real concern is how soon supper will be available because he's hungry. Good mothers, as in this example, are usually automatic in their intuitive understanding of their child. After greeting her son, she offers him a cookie or another snack to tide him over until supper. The following schematic diagram illustrates this basic concept of decoding and encoding messages.[11]

All communication involves encoding, or converting messages into code. We seldom speak entirely honestly with each other but tend to cushion our messages, often increasing the potential for misinterpretation by the receiver. The listener must decode a message to discover its intended meaning.

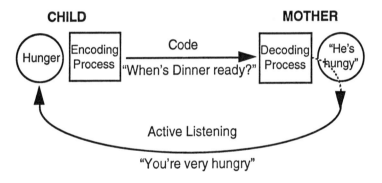

III

COMMUNICATING TO HELP SOLVE PROBLEMS

My dear brothers, take note of this: Everyone
should be quick to listen, slow to speak, and slow to
become angry, for man's anger does not bring about
the righteous life that God desires.

James 1:19

If our usual methods of communication are not effective means of communicating with our children, what should we do? Dr. Gordon suggests the process of decoding a message, called *active listening*. In active listening, one concentrates on decoding to truly hear the intended message. Gordon maintains that parents can help keep youngsters or adults talking and further clarifying their message through the use of "door openers." Here are a few examples of simple door openers:[12]

"I see."	"Really."
"Oh."	"You don't say."
"Mm hmmm."	"No fooling."

"How about that."   "You did, huh?"
"Interesting."   "Is that so!"

Other door openers are more specific in their invitation to give more information:

"Tell me about it."
"I'd like to hear about it."
"Tell me more."
"I'd be interested in your point of view."
"Would you like to talk about it?"
"Let's discuss it."
"Let's hear what you have to say."
"Tell me the whole story."
"Shoot — I'm listening."
"Sounds like you've got something to say about this."
"This seems like something important to you."

These invitations to provide more information encourage the sender to keep talking and help to minimize interference that occurs when the receiver interjects his or her own feelings and thoughts. Door openers convey acceptance and respect, confirming that a child has a right to express how he or she feels, that his or her opinion is valued, and that the listener genuinely cares and is interested in the child.

When children or adults perceive that someone really cares about what they are saying, they know that they are valued. Several years ago, Art Linkletter hosted a program during which he interviewed children before a television audience. He achieved real success in getting children to relate to him simply by using door openers and making children feel he was a truly interested listener. Linkletter bent down to get on the child's eye level, talking to him or her with the same respect he would convey for the President of the United States, giving his undivided attention. The results were marvelous; kids would "say the darndest things" — quite often things their parents had discouraged them from sharing prior to the show. Despite the parental admonitions, the powerful active listening practiced by Art Linkletter paved the way to open communication.

Active listening is a remarkable way to involve the sender with the receiver. Let's return to the schematic diagram used to explain an encoded message.

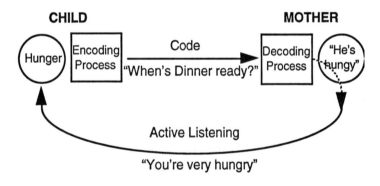

"You're very hungry"

The receiver becomes active by trying to understand what the sender is feeling or what his message really means. To verify his perception, the receiver puts what he heard into his own words and feeds it back to the sender to validate the message. A few examples taken from *Parent Effectiveness Training* will help to illustrate this point:[13]

1. **Child:** *(crying)* Jimmy took my truck away from me.
   Parent: You sure feel bad about that — you don't like it when he does that.
   Child: That's right.

2. **Child:** I don't have anyone to play with since Sally went on vacation with her family. I just don't know what to do for fun without her.
   Parent: You miss having Sally to play with, and you're wondering what you might do to have some fun.
   Child: Yeah. Wish I could think of something.

3. **Child:** Boy, do I have a lousy teacher this year. I don't like him. He's an old grouch.
   Parent: Sounds like you are really disappointed with your teacher.
   Child: I sure am.

4. **Child:** Dad, guess what? I made the basketball team.
   Parent: You're really feeling great about that.
   Child: Am I!

5. **Child:** Daddy, when you were a boy what did you like in a girl? What made you really like a girl?
   Parent: Sounds like you're wondering what you need to get boys to like you, is that right?
   Child: Yeah. They don't seem to like me, and I don't know why.

Notice that the receiver is careful to decode the message without judging or evaluating it. At first, this style of interaction seems strange to those of us who usually communicate in other ways. However, with continual practice, it will seem more natural. If successfully done, active listening can promote a warm parent-child relationship, facilitate problem-solving, and help the child become more receptive to his or her parent's thoughts and ideas.

Active listening can often help us in problem solving, but it will not exempt parents from having problems with their youngsters. Let's turn our attention now to the issue of problem-solving. First and foremost is to understand when a problem is a problem and to determine who should own or be responsible for the problem. Parents often allow problems that should be the responsibility of their children to become theirs, preventing them from assuming responsibility and changing problem-causing behaviors.

Before we can understand problem ownership, a few basic concepts related to acceptability of behaviors must be addressed. Let's turn again to Gordon's *Parent Effectiveness Training* for a better understanding of these concepts. Problem behaviors can be illustrated by the following:[14]

```
+-----------------------------+
|                             |
|            ALL              |
|         POSSIBLE            |
|         BEHAVIORS           |
|                             |
+-----------------------------+
```

If a child's life is represented by the box above, then

all of that child's behaviors fall inside that structure. Some behaviors are acceptable to parents (okay behaviors), while other behaviors are not (not okay behaviors). In the next illustration, a dotted line separates okay and not okay behaviors. The boundary is dotted because it moves depending on the situation.

Okay Behaviors
- - - - - - - - - - -
Not Okay
Behaviors

Area of Acceptable
Behaviors
- - - - - - - - - - - - - - - - - - -
Area of Not
Acceptable
Behaviors

To demonstrate how a behavior's acceptability can change depending on the situation, let's examine the behavior of screaming.

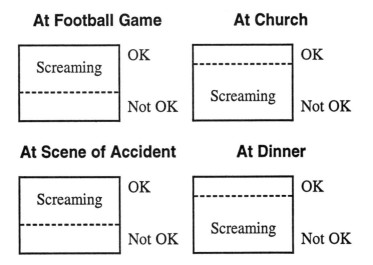

At Football Game

Screaming — OK
- - - - - - - - - - — Not OK

At Church

- - - - - - - - — OK
Screaming — Not OK

At Scene of Accident

Screaming — OK
- - - - - - - - - - — Not OK

At Dinner

- - - - - - - - — OK
Screaming — Not OK

Also, some parents have different standards or levels of tolerance than others. Some are overly accepting or permissive while others are less accepting and more restrictive.

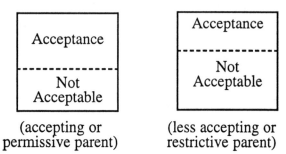

(accepting or permissive parent)   (less accepting or restrictive parent)

Both extremes can be problematic. The overly accepting parent is somewhat neglectful in setting expectations and teaching children societal standards, the difference between right and wrong, and other Christian values. The less accepting parent risks being seen as a rigid, unemotional, uncaring ,and dictatorial, thus laying the foundation for a poor parent-child relationship. Obviously, parents should formulate positions that take into account the age of the child and normal expectations of behavior for that age group.

The boundary lines in the acceptance-nonacceptance box are also dotted, implying that they too move as the situation demands. Parents are likely to be more accepting of their children when they feel energetic and healthy and are content with themselves. Parents who have low self-esteem and are angry, hostile, disappointed, or tired are usually less accepting of their children.

Problems can arise from okay behaviors, but they

usually stem from not okay behaviors. Discovering who is responsible for the problem quite often reveals what, if anything, one can do to resolve it. For example, if the child owns the problem, parents must insist that the child take responsibility for solving it. If the parent owns it partially, the parent can take responsibility for solving only that portion. The important principle here is that the owner of the problem must assume responsibility for solving the problem. No one else should solve the problem without the owner sanctioning that resolution. A further schematic diagram illustrates problem ownership:[15]

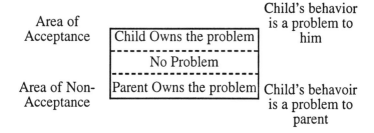

Area of Acceptance	Child Owns the problem	Child's behavior is a problem to him
	No Problem	
Area of Non-Acceptance	Parent Owns the problem	Child's behavoir is a problem to parent

When the child owns a problem, parents should graciously encourage their child to utilize his or her inner resources to solve the problem. This does not imply that parents can't show concern or offer help; parents can always facilitate the resolution of a child's problems. We just need to avoid taking over, which excuses the child from responsibility. Many parents make the mistake of taking full responsibility for problems and dictating a solution. To do so robs children of the important learning experience that struggling to solve a problem provides; it also insults their intelligence by conveying that we don't believe they can solve problems on their own. Furthermore, if we always jump in to solve our children's problems, we foster dependence rather than independence and the ability to make good decisions.

Active listening can greatly enhance the effectiveness parents have as *helping agents*, which is probably much different than the assistance we usually give to our children. The following excerpt illustrates a typical parent-child problem-solving situation:[16]

> **Jason:** Tommy won't play with me today. He won't ever do what I want to do.
>
> **Mother:** Well, why don't you offer to do what he wants to do? You've got to learn to get along with your little friends. *(advising, moralizing)*
>
> **Jason:** I don't like to do the things he wants to do, and besides, I don't want to get along with that dope.
>
> **Mother:** Well, go find someone else to play with then if you're going to be a spoilsport. (offering solution, name-calling)
>
> **Jason:** He's the spoilsport, not me. And there isn't anyone else to play with.
>
> **Mother:** You're just upset because you're tired. You'll feel better about this tomorrow. *(interpreting, reassuring)*
>
> **Jason:** I'm not tired, and I won't feel different tomorrow. You just don't understand how much I hate the little squirt.
>
> **Mother:** Now stop talking like that! If I ever

hear you talk about one of your friends like that again, you'll be sorry. *(ordering, threatening)*

Jason:*(walking away, sulking)* I hate this neighborhood. I wish we would move.

The same scenario with active listening follows:[17]

Jason: Tommy won't play with me today. He won't ever do what I want to do.

Mother: You're kinda angry with Tommy. *(active listening)*

Jason: That's right. But if I don't have him for a friend, I won't have anyone to play with.

Mother: You would hate to be left with no one. *(active listening)*

Jason: I never used to be mad at him, but that's when he was always willing to do what I wanted to do. He won't let me boss him around anymore.

Mother: Tommy's not so easy to influence now. *(active listening)*

Jason: He sure isn't. He's not such a baby now. He's more fun, though.

Mother: You really like him better this way. *(active listening)*

Jason: Yeah. But it's hard to stop bossing him — I'm so used to it. Maybe we wouldn't fight so much if I let him have his way once in a while. Think that would work?

Mother: You're thinking that if you might give in occasionally, it might help. *(active listening)*

45

Jason: Yeah, maybe it would. I'll try it.

Active listening requires us to stay in tune with our own feelings and not allow them to creep into our communication. Most parents communicate nonacceptance by sending "you-messages" to their children:[18]

> You stop that.
> You shouldn't do that.
> Don't you ever…
> If you don't stop that, then…
> Why don't you do this?
> You are naughty.
> You're acting like a baby.
> You want attention.
> Why don't you be good?
> You should know better.

A further example utilizing the following schematic diagram helps to understand the difference between you-message and I-messages[19] (see diagrams on pg 47).

Rather than sending a you-message, communication experts promote what is called an I-message. The sender of an I- message concentrates on his or her personal feelings without judging or criticizing someone else. One can feel judged or attacked by a you-message, but that risk is far less with an I-message, which conveys how the sender feels. Such a message usually stimulates further discussion. A you-message usually closes the door to further discussion, making the recipient defensive, angry, and causing withdrawal from the interaction or an attack. Adults send predominantly

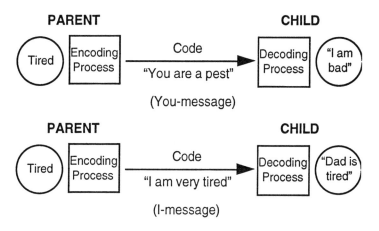

you- messages to their children, which connotes disrespect, appears condescending, and sets up power struggles that no one wins. The following examples help to clarify I-messages:[20]

> "I cannot rest when someone is crawling on my lap."
>
> "I don't feel like playing when I'm tired." "I can't cook when I have to walk around pots and pans on the floor."
>
> "I'm worried about getting dinner ready on time." "I sure get discouraged when I see my clean kitchen dirty again."

Lastly, and probably the most important, a simple problem-solving framework will help parents resolve problems with their children and teach them a logical problem-solving method to use in future situations. Children may need a model that is presented in steps that help break down the process and lead to a successful solution. If used consistently in an open, caring home atmosphere based on love and mutual respect, a problem-solving framework can reduce parent-child conflicts. A suggested model follows:

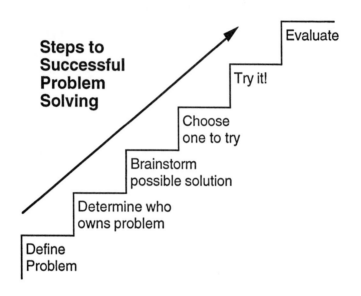

Steps to Successful Problem Solving

Define Problem

Determine who owns problem

Brainstorm possible solution

Choose one to try

Try it!

Evaluate

Parents may also find that reference to the "ladder of success" may be helpful in encouraging their children to strive for success in problem solving. The difference between "I won't" and "I did" is a large one. Children should be challenged to be successful at 70 percent or above. Reference to such visual aids can help children understand the importance of the effort they need to exert in accomplishing their goals or understanding expectations placed on them by their parents.

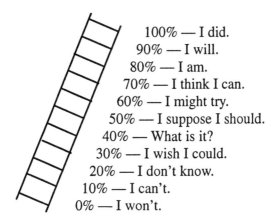

100% — I did.
90% — I will.
80% — I am.
70% — I think I can.
60% — I might try.
50% — I suppose I should.
40% — What is it?
30% — I wish I could.
20% — I don't know.
10% — I can't.
0% — I won't.

IV

UNDERSTANDING YOUR CHILDREN

Then you will understand the fear of the Lord and
find the knowledge of God.
Proverbs 2:5

Parents may make the mistake of trying to understand a child's behavior rather than the child. Art Linkletter told a story about a little girl who lived in an orphanage. Apparently, when she was assigned to the facility, very little background was provided to the staff. Her behavior greatly concerned staff members; she did not relate to or communicate with anyone — neither peers or adults. Despite the many attempts to communicate with her, all efforts seemed fruitless. There didn't seem to be any explanation for the child's behavior, which continued to perplex the staff because she was so different from other children they had served.

Finally, in desperation, a special meeting was called, which included all the staff who had worked with the girl since her admission to the facility. This group of professionals, which included her teacher, house parents, counselor, and, of course, the psychologist, met to review her case. To them the child seemed secretive and manipulative; her behavior did not appear to be normal. After some deliberation, it was decided to place her on 24-hour-a-day observation in an effort to find some clue that might help them further understand what seemed to be significant problems.

Several days passed, but still no answers became apparent. Then one day the girl was playing in the yard with other students. She looked around the playground as if to see whether anyone was watching her, slipped away from the group, and proceeded toward a grove of trees behind the building. Cautiously, the teacher on duty watched her every movement from around the corner of the building. Consistent with the staff's assumptions about the girl's secrecy and manipulation, the teacher speculated that the child had perhaps stolen something from one of her peers or off the teacher's desk and was attempting to hide it. Looking about again to ensure no one was watching, the girl reached into her pocket and then carefully placed what she had removed on the lower limb of a tree. She then hurried back to join the rest of the children, who never noticed her absence.

The teacher hurried toward the tree, thinking how proud of her the administrator and the rest of the staff would be for solving this puzzling case. The teacher quickly retrieved the object from the tree — a small piece of paper that had been carefully folded several times. Hurriedly opening it, the teacher realized that it was a note written in the little girl's own handwriting: "Whoever finds this, I love you!"

The underlying cause of the little girl's behavior was much different than the adults observing her wanted to believe. Once her behavior was better understood, what was previously judged as misbehavior was redefined as meaningful behavior. We often misunderstand our children's behavior because we fail to listen. We are quick to diagnose or judge but slow to listen. One child conveyed this point well:

Listen

When I ask you to listen to me and you start giving advice, you have not done what I asked.

When I ask you to listen to me and you begin to tell me why I shouldn't feel this way, you are trampling on my feelings.

When I ask you to listen to me and you feel you have to do something to solve my problems, you have failed me, strange as that may seem.

Perhaps that's why prayer works for some people.

Because God is mute and He doesn't offer advice or try to fix things, He just listens and trusts you to work it out for yourself.

So please, just listen and hear me.

And if you want to talk, wait a few minutes for your turn and I promise I'll listen to you.

Author Unknown

Far too often we try to understand the behavior we

observe, become frustrated with our lack of understanding, and many times give up rather than concentrate our attention on the child and our relationship. By understanding the child first, we can then better understand his or her behavior.

Further understanding comes with knowledge! Most parents are so overwhelmed by the misbehaviors they fear will embarrass them in public that they take little time to compare the behavior with age-appropriate norms. Some behaviors should be expected and will, with time, take care of themselves. However, many of us cannot stand the thought of allowing our children to be anything but angelic in the eyes of others, especially our friends and family. We place so much pressure on them to comply with our wishes that we destroy their trust, becoming dictators rather than facilitators in the growing-up process. Sometimes we expect too much — other times not enough! Goals should be commensurate with the capacity of a given age or developmental stage to ensure children's success. Many parents get frustrated when their children fail, but the expectations may be too much or too high. Success should be built into reasonable goals that challenge the child but are still achievable.

The following is an abbreviated list of normal developmental expectations adapted from Gesell Institute of Human Development. This list can be used by parents to help them better understand their children and age-appropriate behaviors. These descriptions of behavior represent average developmental levels based on norms for the age group. Individual differences are to be expected. The following charts identify expected behaviors for preschool children aged two to five years followed by descriptions of normal behaviors from age six through late adolescence:[21]

PRESCHOOL CHILDREN

Socially — Personal behavior in relation to other children, adults and groups

2 years	3 years	4 years	5 years
Run-about	Daring	Finding out	Dependable
Self-centered	Desires to please	Self-assertive	Self-assurance and conformability
Negativism - "no"	Socializes his behavior	Independent and sociable	Ready for community experience
Enjoys solitary play	Likes parallel types of play	Forms friendships	"Silliness" and "show-off"
Contacts playmates physically	Resents being helped - "do it myself"	Longs to play with other children	Capacity for friendship
Conforms domestically	Cooperative play sketchy	"Bossiness"	Protective toward younger playmates, siblings
Stands and watches other children play	Can be bargained with	Awareness of attitudes and opinion of others	Can respect authority of those who supervise him
Something of a "dawdler"	Interest in persons	Shares possessions	Can be cooperative and self-reliant
	Girls ahead	Helps around house, short errands, feeds pets, dusts, etc.	

PRESCHOOL CHILDREN

Physically — Motor Characteristics, Routine Needs, Specific Skills

2 years	3 years	4 years	5 years
Runs more than he walks	Likes active large muscle play	More refined and precise gestures	Controlled, mature sense of balance
Tastes of an acrobat	Bowel and bladder control established	Buttons clothes, laces shoes, toilets self, washes hands without help	Dresses self, brushes teeth, combs hair
Likes to fill and empty cans, etc., with sand, water	Feeds self with spoon and small fork, can open door, turn faucet on and off	Likes to climb, balance, jump	Precision and command of tools
Likes to knock down blocks	Helps to bathe self, can hop on one foot	Goes up and down stairs, using alternate feet	Can jig, hop, skip to rhythm changes
Grasps spoon between thumb and index finger	runs, digs, climbs, and jumps	Can climb a tree and come down by self	Laces and ties shoes, skates
Messy or spotless eater	Can ride bike	Independent in eating	
Goes upstairs both feet on each step	Will help set table		
Helps dress self			
Can ride kiddi-car			

56

PRESCHOOL CHILDREN

Mentally — Language, Curiosity, Investigation, Exploration, Questions

2 years	3 years	4 years	5 years
Motor minded	Materialistic	Imaginative	Concrete
Acquires words	Converses	Sophisticated	Speaks distinctly and complete sentences
Chatters happily	Interested in color, texture, music & rhythms	Verbal assertiveness and exaggeration	Perception of order, form, detail
Short attention span			
Likes to investigate and touch things with hands, mouth	"Why"	Tells original story-mixing the truth and fiction	Some sense of time
"Where" "What"	Asks questions about God, death, sex, etc.	Does not like to repeat	Realistic
Knows night and day	Counts two objects	Knows afternoon from morning - yesterday from tomorrow	Asks for information
Names objects	Repeats short sentences		Enjoys humor, laughs heartily at funny pictures
Listens to stories with pictures over and over again	Tells simple stories of daily happenings	Enjoys simple folk and fairy tales	Knows colors
	Knows name and address	Can count to 10	Can carry a tune

57

PRESCHOOL CHILDREN

Emotionally — Feelings of affection, anger, fear, jealousy, anxiety and sympathy

2 years	3 years	4 years	5 years
Selfish	Easily stirred (temper, fears)	Sociable	Reliable
Self-centered		Sophisticated	Stable, well adjusted
Lacks control	Outbursts brief, but he can feel prolonged anxiety	Many fears persist	Innocent of certain complex emotions
Cries easily, frequent outbursts of anger		Senses right and wrong	Capable of anxiety and unreasonable fears
Shows affection spontaneously	Capable of jealousy	Confusion of truth	Transfer of affection from mother to father
Cries when he fails to do what he wants to do	Apt to be possessive	Beginning of pity—"sorry" for others	Loves to receive
Shy with strangers	Likes friendly verbal humor	Learning sense of values (right, wrong, good, bad)	
	Can hold himself in anticipation	Likes to dramatize	

SIX YEAR OLD
Tumultous — Emotional

Very difficult period from 5 1/2 to 6 1/2... this six year old is very much like the two year old.

Violently emotional... loves one minute and hates the next. Feelings are extreme and intense.

Mother is no longer the center of his world... **He Is**!

Wants everything first: must be first at everything and have the most... Mother gets blamed for everything regardless of the circumstances...

Unable to accept criticism, blame, or punishment...

He has to be right. He has to be praised. He has to win.

With others, the six year old is rigid and unadaptable... he has to have things done his own way... others must give into him...

If he is winning he is fine; if not, tears and accusations that others are cheating.

If things going well: warm, enthusiastic, eager, ready for anything... If things going badly: tears and tantrums

Eating: Perpetual motion and unpredictable... tremendous appetite... eyes bigger than his stomach... breakfast usually most difficult meal...may experience nausea at breakfast... intake increases as day goes on. Demands sizeable bed time snack and may awaken during the night hungry. Not able to sit still at meal times and is constant motion.

Sleeping: Beginning to have dreams about death, ghosts, and skeletons - also has good dreams as well... boys generally dream about fires; girls dream of injury to mother...

Elimination: Mostly responsible... may have to make last minute dash... if he has an accident he is very upset about it... Bed Wetting: boys slower to master night time control than are girls...check family history as to when parents gained control and other siblings...

Tension Outlets: Generally restless and clumsy; falls over a piece of string... sits on the edge of his chair and may fall off repeatedly... temper tantrums return... spitting and stuttering...

Fears: Very fearful, especially of noises... fear of supernatural (ghosts and witches)... fears someone under his bed... fear of the elements (fire, water, thunder)... fears sleeping alone or being only one on a floor of the house... fears others will hit him brave about big hurts, but fears splinters, little cuts, nose drops, etc...

Sexuality: Strong interest in origin of babies... interested in how baby gets out of mother and if this hurts... some interest in how baby started... increased awareness and interest in sexual differences and many questions... mild sex play (play doctor) and exhibitionism in play and school toilets...

Parent/Child Relationships: Relationship with mother falls apart... mother primary target for anger and rejection... relationship with father usually much better than ever before... time when father is more effective parent and needs to be involved in child's routines as well as trips to doctors, dentists, school etc...

Siblings: Boss, fight, hurt, and tattle on younger siblings... instigates and likes to see younger siblings punished... fights with older siblings with much pestering and refusing to listen to older siblings who may be left to baby sit...

SEVEN YEAR OLD
Mopey and Moody

The seven year old is more withdrawn, calmer, easier to live with, but more complaints.

Withdraws from conflict and people... likes to be alone... wants own room.

More interest in nonparticipatory activities: TV, radio, reading, electronic games

Fears: The 7 year old's fears are often stimulated by the news... many fears, especially visual: dark, attic, cellar, shadows... fears wars, spies, burglars, people hiding... worries a great deal: being late for school, not being liked...

Sexuality: Wants a baby in the family... knows babies are repeated and that older women don't have them... interest in mother's pregnancy and baby's growth... interest in books about source of babies... generally satisfied with brief and factual explanation...

Parent/Child Relationship: Feels parents do not like him...fantasies of rich parents and adoption... moody with mother and much sulking... less positive relationship with father than at 6, however may worship father and confide in him...

Siblings: Quieter, slightly improved relationship...compare privileges... like role of oldest sibling... some teasing...

School: Cranky and tired… complains… worries particularly about unknown teacher… needs personal support… more dependent on teacher… boys fall in love with teacher and give presents… hard to finish things… sensitive to praise and criticism… doesn't respond quickly and often detours…

Eᴵᴳʜᴛ Yᴇᴀʀ Oʟᴅ
Vigorous

The eight year old is ready to go out into the world... nothing is too difficult.. meets challenges but generally over estimates his abilities... energy sometimes followed by failure and tears: "I always do it wrong."

Speedy... busy... new things... friends... dramatizes...

Needs protection from self-criticism and doing too much...

Interest in both sides of a relationship and it is important to know what other people think...

Demands closeness, especially from mother... expects more from others...

Beginning to get a hint as to the kind of person this child will be...

Bedtime: Still may be an issue - many times bedtime is improved with limited use of a radio or music... beginning to resist parental authority and may choose bedtime as issue...

Dreams: Dreams often are about swimming, flying, movement... scary dreams can usually be traced to TV, books, stories, and parents can help control these by limit setting on such activities prior to bed time...

Fears: Fewer fears… less worried… less fear of the dark… less fear of school…

Sexuality: Understands slow growth process… wants to know where baby is and is confused by the role of mother's stomach… information from parents preferred to from books… girls are more likely to ask about father's role… interest in sex play is high… dirty jokes and profanity increase… sex play often occurs if children left unsupervised with nothing to do… sex play needs to be approached calmly and treated as other behaviors are approached…

Parent/Child Relationships: Child haunts mother… wants mother to think the same as he does and is sensitive to her approval… wants to meet mother's standards… first deep relationship for the child… less intense relationship with the father and is able to accept father's making mistakes… jealous of mother/father relationship… will respond to a mind father better…

Siblings: Problems increase… teasing, selfishness… some interest in family background…

School: Eight year old enjoys school… very major need to communicate and to express his opinion… especially responsive to praise… generally obeys, however may argue first… immediate rewards help… no longer wants detailed directions (babyish)

NINE YEAR OLD
Thoughtful and Mysterious

Ready for anything... demands to be extremely independent... friends and peers become more important than family... resists too much "bossing" from parents... looks at adults from interest in what they can do for him and not interested in the relationship... can't impose yourself on a nine year old... if treated as the mature creature he thinks he is, he gets along pretty well and can be fairly self-reliant and capable.

The nine year old can be a worrier... takes things too seriously... can be extremely anxious and may go to pieces over minor things... much worry and complaining - rather neurotic age...

Nine year old will complain of tasks being difficult, both at home and school... many complaints of physical discomfort: stomach aches, eyes hurt, etc. Remember, the discomfort is real... usually the discomfort and complain go together: eyes hurt when he has to read; stomach hurts when he has to rake the yard; hands hurt when he has to practice the piano; has to go to the bathroom when he has to do the dishes.

Nine is an age of rebellion: passively and complaining

Eating: Generally no problems - may refuse to eat meats
and chicken - particularly fats

Sleeping: Usually area to challenge parent's authority and may need to negotiate a later bedtime - appeal to his maturity, i.e. no stalling or complaining and getting up in the morning without difficulties...

Tension Outlets: Physical complaints... stamping feet... playing with buttons on shirt, dress, or coat... drops and breaks things... growling and muttering... feels dizzy...

Fears: Fears are reasonable... generally concerned with personal failure and his inabilities... many fears will focus on school performance...

Sexuality: Most know about menstruation... interest in father's role of reproduction... more appreciation of books on the subject... interested in the differences between sexes however move away from the opposite sex - much swapping of sexual information... seek sexual pictures in books... beginning sexual swearing and poems...

Parent/Child Relationship: Suddenly friends are more important than family... many times this is real loss for mother and there is temptation to deal with this be excessive demands and directions... time to reduce unnecessary commands and directives... children competitive regarding parents' occupations and father a bit more important than in the past...

TEN YEAR OLD
Peaceful

For the ten year old, parents' word is law... all of his choices are presented in terms of his parents' sanctions or limits... "yes, Mom say I can," or "No, my parents won't let me."

He obeys easily and naturally and expects to gain status by his obedience. Not only does he obey, but he is pleased with his family and parents in general... He is nice and friendly to others.

The ten year old is matter-of-fact and straight forward... flexible... doesn't take things too seriously...

Ten is an age of predictability and comfortable equilibrium... adults receive whole hearted and unreserved acceptance...

Eating: Continues to increase in appetite... 10 year old even dreams of food... not a time to consider diets unless the child is grossly overweight... has not yet made association between food eaten and weight gain.

Sleeping: Usually no problems associated with bed time or sleeping.

Tension Outlets: Same as nine year old...

Fears: Many fears... animals, especially snakes and wild animals... also fears high places, fires, criminals...

beginning to mention things they are not afraid of, i.e. dark and being alone...

Sexuality: Knowledge level and sexual interest similar to nine year old - will begin to tell and have some basic understanding of "dirty jokes..."

Parent/Child Relationships: Happy and conforming... parents know best... many not follow directions immediately, but will comply... high point of father/child relationship... father can do no wrong...

ELEVEN – THIRTEEN

Children vary greatly during this age range... generally they are similar in terms of developmental process.

Time of great physical and behavioral change which ends with puberty...

Physiological growth intensifies... increase in hormones... many inner tensions... boys sometimes feel masculinity threatened and may react with aggressive behaviors...

Body movements express their attitudes about their bodies... many are disharmonious and gangly... the body is the focus of most attention... deviations from the development of peers causes feelings of inferiority...

Friends become more important and help deal with upsets and help them to externalize their feelings... allows closeness to peers, not parents... girls interested in rock stars, boys interested in athletes, these may be adults, but does not include parents...

ADOLESCENCE
14 – 16 Years

Social Development

Family: Overt expression of independence requires acceptance and facilitation...Possible conflict over restrictions on driving... may resent limitations imposed...

Peers: Preoccupation with acceptance by social group... intimate and casual heterosexual activity and experimentation occur... boys and girls have a few close friends of both sexes; friendships last longer... increase in conflict between peer and adult roles... independent judgement emerges despite tendency to conformity... girls continue to be more socially adept than boys... primary groups continue to be same sex, but more heterosexual, interaction... peer group influences greatly intensified...

School: Plans for investigates career choices... strongly expresses opinions and beliefs which may be contrary to those of school personnel...

Self Development

Emotions: Competitive peer relationships produce some distrust... daydreaming is common... confides more in friends than in parents... assurance of acceptance and security from parents is still necessary... emotional energy continues to be expanded toward physical change and developing heterosexual relationships... worries about physical appearance, attractiveness and physical development...

Values: Interest in philosophical, ethical, and religious problems... is aware of and verbalizes contradictions in moral code... group beliefs important in influencing values...

Self: Achieving independence from parents... developing socially responsible behavior and achieving new and more mature relations with age mates of both sexes...

Thinking/Language Development

Thinking: Makes fine conceptual distinctions... concerned with the hypothetical, the future and the remote... increased capacity for planning; consider long-range purposes... formulates and tests hypotheses to consider all possible ways a problem can be solved; deals with logical and imaginary solutions... aspirations frequently exceed capabilities uses abstract rules to solve problems...

Language: Should be able to use language to express and clarify complex concepts...

Physical Development

Adolescent growth spurt at peak for boys, with changes

in body proportions, resulting in awkwardness... pubescent stage for boys: secondary sex characteristics continue to develop... early or late physical maturing has less impact on girls than on boys, especially in regard to self concept...

ADOLESCENCE
17 – 19 Years

Social Development

Family: Parental advice and support important in transition to adulthood, i.e. career, economic, and marital decisions... may be leaving home for extended period... enjoys freedom, but feels doubts... with more freedom, makes more independent judgements regarding alcohol, drugs, etc...

Peers: Choice and decisions reflect continuing peer influence... exploring possibilities of becoming more desirable as a mate... group activities provide an outlet for expressing feelings... may be living full time with peers in a college setting; new interpersonal satisfactions and problems...

School: Has responsibility for decisions to be made in post-high school education...

Self Development

Emotions: Worries about career choice and other aspects of future... anxious about formulation and continuation of intimate heterosexual relationships... may be experiencing a wholehearted love affair...

Values: Integration of values into a personal philosophy including ethical and moral standards to be used in adult life... is able to make a personal commitment to causes...

Self: Moves toward permanence in job choice, training, education... looking for permanence in intimate relationships... looking for assurance regarding future economic security... may be directly involved in own marital and family life decisions...

Thinking/Language Development

Thinking: Continues to refine language and thinking abilities... increased life experiences provide more and new opportunities for refinement of previously learned reasoning-thinking skills...

Language: Inadequate language skills may adversely affect job opportunities and limit career choices...

Physical Development

Full physical development for both boys and girls... most boys and girls have had physical contact of a sexual nature... both sexes are struggling to learn socially approved outlets for sexual arousal...

V

WORKING AS A TEAM

Make every effort to keep the unity of the spirit
through the bond of peace.
Ephesians 4:3

Most parents would agree that one important element in a winning football season is teamwork. It has often been said that teamwork is even more important than a good coaching staff. If the team is strong, it can be successful regardless of the coaching. The opposite is also true in that no matter how good the coaching, if the team is weak, it may never see success. The team that doesn't apply good teamwork principles becomes a group without common goals and usually doesn't make it to the play-offs.

Parents must follow the same principles that teams

do to be successful in reaching their goals. Successful parenting, even if you apply all the important concepts described in this book, doesn't happen automatically. To maximize the chance for success, both mom and dad must work together and have common goals. There is comfort in difficult times when you have support from a partner. Roles, responsibilities, and necessary commitments can be shared, thus making the often arduous task of parenting more enjoyable and perhaps even more successful. During a crisis, it is always nice to know that you are not facing that little monster or big monster, whatever the case may be, by yourself.

Teamwork is one of the most fundamental concepts of parenting. It's more than a set of skills — it's an attitude! We can adopt this attitude by attempting to share equally in the responsibilities as well as the joys of parenting. Many a young father passes out his birth announcements and proudly shows his newborn pictures to fellow workers and friends, however, then leaves the ongoing tasks of raising that child to his wife. He may show renewed interest during the little league years to take pride in his son's accomplishments but is uninvolved with anything other than sports. All of parenting must be shared, not just selected events or stages. It is easy to parent during the good times. The more difficult challenges are just as important, since successful parenting during these times will help us face future challenges that test our resources and tend to be anything but rewarding experiences.

Perhaps the concept of teamwork can be best understood by breaking the word down as follows:

T...ogether
E...ach
A...ccomplishes
M...ore

Teamwork implies that each member of the team is a contributing member. By contributing the skills one possesses, each member strengthens the team. Combined efforts mean more resources and creativity. Parents must support each other in their parenting responsibilities. Rather than be critical of each other, they must give each other support. Mutual respect of team members is of utmost importance. Respect not only maintains good team spirit and high morale; it has learning value for children who see their parents modeling cooperation and performing as a team.

If parents truly accept the need for teamwork and work together in rearing children, there is absolutely no challenge beyond their capabilities. Parents can combine their resources of intelligence, experience, and creativity to deal with just a few years of the child's mischief and manipulation. Parents can always outfox their children if they combine their resources. This, of course, implies that problems and the responsibility for solving them are shared.

Practicing teamwork may not yield perfection, but it brings parents closer to success. No one accomplishes good teamwork overnight. Attaining this skill may take several months or even years. The more people truly practice it, the better they become. A good coach schedules several practice sessions prior to a game, which helps to increase team members' confidence.

If teamwork is the answer to good parenting, how does one go about developing it? First of all, teamwork must be understood as a willingness to work together in harmony. Parents must have a cooperative attitude if they are to be a team. Team members who play as individuals have a difficult time formulating common goals and working together to accomplish those goals. Yet we tend to go about our parenting tasks as if we are doing shift work. Instead of pooling our resources, we work independently. Parents must have a commitment to work together. They may not always agree on everything, but they must have a commitment to cooperate. It is virtually impossible for two adults to agree on every issue of parenting for their children. There must be willingness to compromise and to blend opinions by consensus into something they can both support. Modeling how differences are resolved, compromises are made, and teams are made stronger than individuals who comprise them teaches children by example.

Teamwork is probably better understood if we break it down into its component parts: technical skills and interpersonal skills. Technical skills involve good parenting techniques, or the how-to methods. Being consistent, setting priorities, communicating effectively, implementing good discipline rather than punishment, and good decision making are all important technical skills. Technical skills can be learned through practice. Interpersonal skills include those that facilitate good relationships and getting along with others: acceptance of constructive criticism, willingness to compromise, openness, respect, tolerance of another person's viewpoint, and positive attitude.

Inconsistency between parents can cause confusion about expectations and will probably frustrate the child. This frustration can lead to rebellion, withdrawal, or even manipulation by using parents' inconsistency to gain control or advantage. Setting mutually agreed-upon priorities and balancing them with other important activities are important technical skills. For example, participation in sports can be very important in building social skills; however, that participation must be balanced with homework and family activities. If grades fall during a sports season and parents ignore academic pursuits, they are telling their children that sports are more important than education.

Obviously, balancing priorities also demands another technical skill — time management. Helping the child manage his or her time in a way that balances priorities is a good lesson that will have greater application as commitments and responsibilities grow. Parents need to practice good decision making and certainly good communication skills that will help to facilitate decision making. Setting priorities will come easier if both parents are able to discuss the important values through good communication. While both parents' participation is important for some things, dividing responsibilities to help balance commitments may prove helpful and make more time for shared family activities.

Aside from making parenting an easier task for parents, teamwork is also important since "teamwork" provides a good model of cooperation for children. Research on how children learn has suggested that most of a child's behavior is acquired by watching other people do the behavior and then imitating through modeling.[22] In regard to modeling, James Dobson says that children "catch" more things than they are taught directly. A good teacher recognizes the importance of providing experiential situations in which students can apply knowledge. Sometimes, seeing a skill demonstrated makes learning that skill much easier. Seeing a principle in action can help a child understand it.

If you ever want to amuse yourself in a shopping mall, just take a few minutes and observe people. Find a youngster of toddler age and an accompanying parent and observe how the youngster tries to mimic the adult. You'll see the powerful concept of modeling illustrated in real life. As a graduate student several years ago, I would often study at a desk in our family room. Our son was about three years of age. He, too, had a small desk beside mine. He consistently watched me study my various psychology textbooks. As I underscored several lines of important information, he would likewise underscore his books with a pencil in exactly the same manner he had seen me do.

There are certain conditions that motivate a child to model after someone. First of all, the model is usually a "significant other" person for the child. Becoming a significant other for our children does not automatically occur because we are their parents. We earn this distinction by building the kind of relationship previously described. Research has also confirmed that children model after adults they perceive as being competent and having high status, and who reinforce the child for modeling after them.

Achieving high status with our children is not hard when they are at preschool age, but as time goes on, high status comes only with a growing positive relationship based on love, care, concern, and trust. When we reinforce our children for modeling after us, we are obviously rewarding behavior we wish to have repeated, therefore, strengthening that behavior. Children are an excellent source of feedback; they may also reflect less-than-positive behaviors they have seen modeled by us. If a child exhibits a behavior modeled by another source that parents do not wish to have repeated, this problem can be easily remedied by offering alternative modeling. As parents, our influence should be greater than other sources if we have become significant others to our children and maintained the high status parents should strive to keep. By our attitudes and behavior, we provide children with examples of how to react in similar situations.[23]

VI

UNDERSTANDING PUNISHMENT AND DISCIPLINE

Discipline your son, and he will give you peace; he
will bring delight to your soul.
Proverbs 29:17

Probably more than any other area, parents request help with discipline. The majority of parents want ready-made recipes that are guaranteed to work. Unfortunately, there are no such guarantees. We will address some basic principles of discipline, review the differences between punishment and discipline, and address the question of corporal punishment, or spanking, which remains quite controversial with many Christian parents. The next chapter will build on this discussion of principles as well move into considering specific techniques for effective discipline.

As already emphasized, a prerequisite to good

parent-child interactions is *a solid, positive relationship* between parent and child. Without this relationship, there is no authority, and parents resort to intimidation, threats, fear, and other antagonizing means to force or impose their will upon the child. Most children desire to please parents whom they have come to trust and love.

A principle worth repeating is that *problems are opportunities.* Parents must accept that problems are normal for children and a regular challenge for their parenting skills. If we as parents get overwhelmed by our child's misbehavior, we will hardly be in a frame of mind to use this situation to teach the child. Remember that most of us, even as adults, learn best through experience, quite often through our failures or mistakes. Edmund Cooke once said, "Trouble is what you make it." Some parents make misbehavior a much bigger problem and far more trouble than it really is. By making it a catastrophe, they ruin the potential learning that such a situation affords. Each naturally occurring problem provides parents with an opportunity to teach important lessons and values to their children.

Controlling the environment or *making planned changes* in environmental conditions can sometimes alter a behavior without saying anything to the child. Many parents create a home environment that is so restrictive and boring that it invites misbehavior. As the old cliché goes, "Idle hands are the devil's workshop." Children often create their own entertainment by manipulating parents, trying to get away with as much as they can, testing their parents' tolerance and limits, and many other less desirable things that antagonize and test the patience of parents. Children need to know what is expected of them and to have a predictable routine (established bed times, meal times, homework schedule, curfews, etc.). If this type of structure is absent from the home environment, children tend to test their limits. Through "testing behavior," children are asking for limits to be established.

Parents who wish to establish a foundation for good discipline should not underestimate the *power of touch*. Perhaps the following poem by Kathleen Keating summarizes this principle best:[24]

Hugs

There is no such thing as a bad hug:
There are only good hugs and great hugs.
Hug someone at least once a day
and twice on a rainy day.
Hug with a smile; closed eyes are optional.
A snuggle is a longish hug.
Bedtime hugs help chase away bad dreams.
Never hug tomorrow someone
you could hug today.

Much child development research supports the need for touch stimulation for both emotional and physical health. Almost everyone enjoys being touched; this is particularly true of children. Touch can relieve pain, reduce depression and anxiety, and sometimes has positive effects on children's language development and level of intelligence. Parents forget that sometimes behavior can be altered simply by touching a child at the right moment. Many times a child may be subconsciously acting out to get the attention that such a touch provides. We need to be "touch people" when it comes to our children. Touch speaks deeply to the soul, conveying care and concern, love and appreciation, in a way that words cannot accomplish.

This phenomenon of touch is important for another reason — through it children can learn the difference between appropriate touching and inappropriate touching. Sexual abuse of children is increasing in our society. Children who come from homes where touching is not practiced might be at greater risk for abuse by others because they have a need for affection that is unmet in their own homes. When faced with the beginning stages of an abuser's approach, the touching quite often seems harmless to a child. Even though the child may have some ambivalence, the need to be touched and his or her difficulty in discerning the difference between a good and bad touch quite often allows a child to accept an abuser's initial efforts. By the time such touching becomes obviously wrong to the child, it may be too late to avoid its harmful effects. The resulting guilt that such abuse leaves with a child often causes him or her to avoid telling parents.

Before delving into specific disciplinary techniques, we need to examine the differences between discipline and punishment and to look at corporal punishment. Many parents understand discipline and punishment as equal or synonymous, although they are in fact quite different and in many respects are opposites. Discipline is sometimes used to label what a parent punitively administers to a child and which is actually punishment rather than discipline. Discipline is a positive learning experience that sets behavioral limits and guidelines to lead children to adulthood. Punishment quite often is used to hurt by causing physical or psychological pain.[25] Of course, the theory behind punishment is that the child will learn to avoid pain and therefore cease to behave in a manner that results in such a consequence. Discipline, on the other hand, always contains a learning aspect and focuses on internalizing a value, which then helps the child to cease behaviors inconsistent with the internalized value. Discipline can be a positive experience, but punishment is almost always a negative experience with several less-than-desirable consequences.

The Child Discipline Guidelines for Parents set forth the purposes of discipline as follows: (1) to teach children how to achieve for themselves, (2) to lead children to self-discipline so that they will behave properly without parental or adult guidance, and (3) to help children experience pride and pleasure when they do what is right.[26] Thus good parents discipline so that they can facilitate growth of their children toward becoming independent, self-sufficient adults who make responsible decisions. Discipline facilitates growth, learning, and a healthy sense of responsibility; punishment, on the other hand, causes children to feel shame and guilt. Punishment attacks the child's self-esteem, but discipline teaches children how to raise self-esteem by taking responsibility for and control of their behavior.

The National Committee for Prevention of Child Abuse[27] characterizes discipline as helping children control and change their behavior, guiding them into adulthood. It enhances a child's self-worth by treating him or her with respect and taking the time required to help a child learn important lessons. Discipline is best taught by example.[28] The model we provide as parents is a far more effective teaching tool than anything we verbalize — actions speak louder than words!

Just as discipline tends to build a child's self-esteem, punishment tends to destroy it, as well as cause other negative emotional responses such as fear, anxiety, hate, resentment, withdrawal, and isolation. Some argue that punishment does work toward a reduction or complete elimination of the negative behavior that precedes it, therefore justifying it as means to an end. However, one must not be too quick to accept punishment as a viable alternative in parenting without first considering its outcomes.

In a rather dated study, Krumboltz and Krumboltz[29] report that punishment has some serious dangers: (1) attempted punishment may serve as reinforcement, thereby increasing rather than reducing the undesired behavior, (2) children tend to resist punishment by fighting back, actively escaping, or by withdrawing into passive apathy, and (3) a child tends to avoid the punisher whenever he can. Obviously, these drawbacks can seriously hamper the parent-child relationship.

Furthermore, if punishment is upheld, there is no room left for reconciliation. If it is too severe, there is no way to take the punishment back. Finally, even if punishment seems to work, its results will probably be short-lived; the punished child has learned only to avoid a behavior and the subsequent punishment rather than internalize values, understand why such behavior is unacceptable, and then choose more appropriate behaviors. Some children quickly become immune to punishment, making· even short-term effectiveness questionable.

If a parent's role in the home is only to inflict punishment, mistakenly viewed as discipline, the family should not be surprised when the child becomes hateful, distant, sullen, and difficult.[30] Spanking has all of the negative aspects of punishment described above. It can be a violent act that demonstrates using physical force to promote a parent's cause — hardly a social skill we should be teaching our children. It is poor communication in that it is usually imparted in anger, generally offers no explanation, and has many negative ramifications. Spanking does not usually help children internalize any value but simply causes them to suppress the associated behaviors to avoid such response from caregivers.

Spanking is also a poor excuse for parental discipline in that it requires little creativity. Many parents who advocate spanking tend to be somewhat lax in taking responsibility for disciplining their children. They choose spanking because it is quick and easy, and it doesn't require much thinking.

What about Christian parents who advocate physical punishment because they claim it is scriptural? My response is that anyone can quote Scripture to support a practice they wish to justify. The references quoted most often in support of corporal punishment are found in Proverbs:

Proverbs 13:24

> He who spares the rod hates his son,
> but he who loves him is careful to discipline
> him.

Proverbs 22:15

> Folly is bound up in the heart of a child,
> but the rod of discipline will drive it far from
> him.

Proverbs 23:13-14

> Do not withhold discipline from a child;
> if you punish him with the rod, he will not die.
> Punish him with the rod and save his soul from
> death.

Proverbs 29:17

> Discipline your son, and he will give you
> peace;
> he will bring delight to your soul.

The word *correction* or *correct* in the King James Version has been translated as *discipline* in the New International Version. However, in light of our understanding of discipline and punishment, *punishment* would be more appropriate in reference to "beating with a rod."

Those who quote Proverbs as justification for corporal punishment will discount Deuteronomy 13:6-10, which instructs one to stone to death the child who entices anyone to worship another god. Proverbs is a book of "wise old sayings." Deuteronomy is one of the books of the Law. Most would agree that a book of the Law carries more weight than a book of wise old sayings. Yet Proverbs is interpreted literally to support corporal punishment, and Deuteronomy is interpreted figuratively and rejected as not having application in the modern world.

Beyond the selective application of Scripture, one must consider interpretation necessary, especially as when passages are used to address specific issues such as discipline or punishment. Scriptural interpretations are quite often figurative and must always make some transition to modern-day. For example, in biblical days, the rod was not just any pole or stick; it was a symbol of miraculous power. In Psalm 23, the rod symbolizes gentleness: "Your rod and your staff, they comfort me" (v. 4).

Rather than focusing on the proverbs of Solomon, whose life was characterized by poor values and questionable morals, let us turn our attention to the Master: "I tell you the truth, unless you change and become like little children, you will never enter the Kingdom of Heaven" (Matthew 18:3). Perhaps it is said best by The Committee to End Violence Against the Next Generation in its publication *The Bible and the Rod*:[31]

> To Jesus, not only did the grown-ups not have all the answers, but they may have forgotten things that they knew in youth. Many things fade as we depart from childhood. The power to laugh joyfully, to dream and imagine, to love truly, and form deep relationships, to believe in wonders

and sense the things of the Spirit. In teaching youth our knowledge, instead of "beating the foolishness out of them" we may have something to learn in return.

Christ emphasized the importance of children and their importance to Him. In Mark 10:14, we read "Let the little children to come to me, and do not hinder them, for the kingdom of God belongs to such as these." Christ further warns in Luke 17:2 that it would be better for one to have a millstone hung around his neck and be thrown into the sea than to cause a child to sin. Jesus never used force against or caused pain to human beings or to the beasts of the land, and certainly not to children, whom He presented as models of the innocence necessary to please God. Christ represents love:

> There is no fear in love. But perfect love drives out fear, because fear has to do with punishment. The man who fears God is not made perfect in love (1 John 4:18).

Parents are admonished in Ephesians 6:4,"Do not exasperate your children; instead, bring them up in the training and instruction of the Lord." *Exasperate* means "to make more sharp or severe; aggravate, to embitter or irritate.[32] Of course punishment engenders hurt and anger.

Having worked with emotionally disturbed children and their families for a number of years, I have met hundreds of children who have been physically abused by their parents or caregivers — quite often one of the causes for the resulting emotional disturbance. Such children are angry and hostile, and they fear trusting any adult; their anger precludes the ability to love others.

Physical punishment might be appropriate if immediate action is required to prevent a child from participating in a life-threatening behavior, but even then its effectiveness must be weighed against its multiple negative ramifications. For example, if a two-year-old child repeatedly runs into a busy street and the parent has tried unsuccessfully to change this behavior with nonpunitive measures, punishment might be necessary — that behavior must be stopped. A two-year-old child has not developed the cognitive skills that allow him or her to understand the reasoning behind a parent's demand not to play in the middle of a busy street. However, the child can learn that a spanking always follows running into the street. As soon as the child is old enough to reason in simple cognitive terms, it is important to find alternative means of disciplining the child. Physical punishment should only be used as a last resort, and then only in emergency situations as previously described. All other uses of corporal punishment should be seriously questioned and replaced with more creative disciplinary methods in which the goal is internalization of values rather than fear.

John E. Valusek, Ph.D., a psychologist who has studied the effects of punishment on children, presents variations of hitting[33] (see chart on page 93).

As can easily be seen by looking at the effect of each type of stroke, all forms of hitting cause pain. According to our definitions of punishment and discipline, hitting must be classified as punishment, with all the negative ramifications associated with it. Valusek points out that although items 1 through 10 are considered discipline if used by parents or school administrators, these same items (as well as 11 and 12) are called hitting or fighting if done by children to other children.

Valusek further illustrates his concept of hitting with The Yardstick of Violence:

The Yardstick of Violence

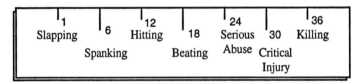

Hitting can be justified as "discipline" all the way across the continuum to murder. When does hitting become hurtful? When it is too hard? When does one begin to question the safety of its recipient? All of these questions are very important to parents who wish to use corporal punishment. As Valusek states, hitting is hitting, no matter how you define it or for what use it may be intended. "People are not for hitting....and children are people, too."[34]

Some Forms and Variations of Hitting

Types of Painful Stroke	Instrument	Usual Label	Effect
1. Single mild slap 2. Repeated mild slaps 3. Single forcefule slap 4. Repeated forceful slaps	Open hand	Slapping or Spanking	Mild to Moderate Pain
5. Single mid strike 6. Repeated mild strikes 7. Single forceful strike 8. Repeated forceful strikes	Switch, Stick, Ruler, Wooden spoon, Hair brush, Fly swatter, or Rolled newspaper	Spanking	Mild to Moderate or Severe Pain
9. Single blow 10. Repeated blows	Belt, Paddle, Rubber hose, Broom handle or electric cord	Spanking, Hitting, Beating or Abuse	Moderate to Severe Pain
11. Single blow 12. Repeated blows	Closed Fist	Hitting, Fighting, Battery, or Abuse	Moderate to Severe Pain
13. Repeated forceful blows	Fists, belts, boards, kicks or blow by any hand-held or thrown object, instrument or weapon	Hitting, Battery, or Severe Abuse	Severe Pain: Usually requires Medical Attention
14. Single or repeated blows	Any instrument, means or weapon which causes death to occur	Killing or Murder	Severe Pain to End of Life

VII

TEACHING RIGHT FROM WRONG WITH DISCIPLINE

Children obey your parents in the Lord, for this is
right. Honor your father and mother which is the
first commandment.
Ephesians 6:1

If physical punishment is not appropriate, then what
is? There are hundreds of substitutes for corporal
punishment; it can truly become the last resort and
need never be used with most children. I will not
attempt to discuss every method, but I will present some
of the more common-sense approaches that have been
found effective. We will look at seven areas: (1)
behavioral approaches, (2) the productive use of
anxiety, (3) reversal of responsibility, (4) logical and
natural consequences, (5) mediation training, and (6)
power struggles and (7) additional miscellaneous
techniques. The chapter will conclude by providing 36

Positive Approaches To Discipline adapted from Saf Lerman's Parent Awareness Traning.

Behavioral Approaches

One could be overwhelmed by all the written material available on behavioral techniques alone. However, the fundamental principle of behavioral psychology is a simple one: reinforcement through reward. A reward is defined as an event or a desirable consequence that immediately follows a behavior, resulting in repetition of the behavior.[35] People tend to repeat behaviors that result in positive rewards. Positive reinforcement can take two forms: social and nonsocial. *Social reinforcement* includes verbal praise, physical gestures of approval and affection, public ceremonial awards in which a child is recognized publicly for behavior or accomplishment, or maybe simply a smile or approving facial expression from a teacher or caregiver. The following example demonstrates social reinforcement:

Praise:	"You're doing a good job."
	"That's excellent."
Approval:	"You're doing very well."
	"I'm proud of you when you do that."
Attention:	A pat on the back, a smile, or a
	"Thank you."
Informational	"That's correct."
Feedback:	"You're following directions well."

Nonsocial reinforcement involves a tangible reward

rather than social interaction or attention. Nonsocial rewards commonly used to reward behavior include such things as candy, tokens, points, money (five dollars for each A on a report card), or any other tangible item that is desired by the child. Quite often, points are accumulated by children to be traded for some tangible reward or highly sought-after recreational activity. Both social and nonsocial rewards usually work well to motivate children of all ages, and they work best if used in combination with each other. Very few children will argue with a system that allows them to work toward something they desire, whether it be an inexpensive package of candy or a trip to a recreational park.

Behavior charts such as the one that follows work well in recording checks or points, which can then be used to reach a goal set by parents or caregivers[36](see page 83).

The concept of *shaping* simply means that parents set up reinforcements for successive approximations, in a step-by-step process until the desired behavior is achieved. For example, for a six- or seven-year-old child to clean his or her own room completely each day before leaving for school might be too overwhelming. However, asking the child to make the bed, hang play clothes on the appropriate closet hook, and place toys in the toy chest are small steps that can be successfully accomplished. Success with small steps leads to the long-range goal of leaving the room in a neat, orderly fashion each morning. It is important for parents to refer to developmental norms and appropriate expectations. Success must be built in so that children feel successful and are motivated to perform these tasks.

The opposite of earning a reward is losing one —

"My Jobs"

November	14	15	16	17	18	19	20	21	22	23	24	25	26	27	28	29	30
1. I brushed my teeth without being told																	
2. I straightened my room before bedtime																	
3. I picked up my clothes without being told																	
4. I fed the fish without being told																	
5. I emptied the trash without being told																	
6. I minded Mommie today																	
7. I minded Daddy today																	
8. I said my prayers tonight																	
9. I was kind to little brother Billy today																	
10. I took my vitamin pill																	
11. I said "thank you" and "please" today																	
12. I went to bed last night without complaining																	
13. I gave clean water to the dog today																	
14. I washed my hands and came to the table when called																	
TOTAL:																	

response cost. While children can earn checks for appropriate behaviors, they could lose some for misbehavior. Although not recommended for frequent use, this approach has a learning component; just as an adult recognizes the importance of driving the speed limit after receiving a speeding ticket , a child learns from response cost. A child might also be given a restriction or grounded, during which time he or she is not permitted to earn privileges or participate in normal activities. This form of discipline or grounding is termed *time out from reinforcement.* This is similar to suspension of a privilege because a child demonstrated a lack of responsibility regarding that specific privilege. For example, a parent might choose to ground a child for a day or two for not coming home at the previously arranged time.

At times, setting up a *written contract* with a child can have a positive effect in motivating behavioral change. For example, if grades are a problem for Chris, the following contract between Chris and his parents might help to bring about change.

Written Contract

I, ___Chris_____, promise to study one
hour each night and try to raise my grades by
one letter grade during this next grading
period. If successful in keeping this promise
of studying and raising the letter grades, it is
agreed that I will receive a bonus of $20 and a
weekend fishing trip with Mom and Dad and
a friend of my choice.

Signed: _____ Date: _____

It is important that the contract conditions be attractive to both parties and stated in simple, understandable terms. The requested change should be easily measured (for example, increase of one letter grade) and aimed at motivating desired changes in behavior.

In using *positive practice,* parents request that a child practice a behavior they wish to see improved. Positive practice not only helps the child know that he or she can accomplish the behavior with some effort but can also serve as a disciplinary approach. For example, if a youngster always forgets to turn off lights when leaving a room, parents might ask the child to practice four or five times to help him or her remember this important lesson in energy conservation. Parents must remember, though, that positive practice should truly be positive. If a child is forced to practice excessively and the focus becomes punitive, then the measure becomes punishment rather than discipline and loses its educational component. Positive practice should *inconvenience* the child by occurring on the child's time, for example, during his or her favorite cartoon or television program. This allows the child to experience the consequences of his or her misbehavior. Practicing bedtime behavior during Saturday morning cartoons usually has overwhelming success in altering undesirable patterns.

Sometimes, parents must simply *ignore* misbehavior. Parents often focus so much attention on misbehavior that they reinforce it rather than correct it, especially if they unknowingly give more attention to misbehavior than they do positive behavior. Some children enjoy any attention, no matter what the reason; they seem to continue misbehaving simply to get their parents' attention.

Another behavioral approach to discipline that works well is offering an *incompatible response* or *redirecting* the child's behavior. While a child is misbehaving, the parent offers another more attractive behavior that is completely incompatible with the behavior he or she is currently exhibiting, thereby forcing the child to make a choice. The more enticing the new behavior is, the better the chances that the child will choose it over the misbehavior. Suppose two siblings are fighting in the family room. Of course, both children have a taste for ice cream cones and would do virtually anything to obtain one. Rather than call attention to the fight, their father announces that he is going out for ice cream and wonders if they cared to join him. They will stop fighting at least long enough to think about their options.

The Productive Use of Anxiety

Anxiety can be a very uncomfortable state, and most people will work toward eliminating it. When anxious, people usually start exploring options that might lower such feelings, and it is this same anxiety that causes many of us to change our behavior. Parents can use anxiety productively by making their children a little uncomfortable or ill at ease about misbehavior. Children need a predictable environment with consistent expectations, for such adds to their security, sense of well being, and feelings of adequacy. However, parents often become too predictable in their discipline; then children experience very little discomfort.

Most parents quickly react and announce the discipline they have chosen for their son or daughter, and by so doing, they do not allow time for the child to contemplate or think about his misbehavior. If parents are too predictable, the child learns quickly how to manipulate the system and quite often decides to misbehave and accept the consequence he knows will follow. A child who knows the system this well has little anxiety over misbehavior. Once having such power or control, the child learns manipulative behaviors which he can then use to control his parents and others as well.

James Dobson tells a story about the father of one of his boyhood friends. The father, a church board member, swore when he became angry. The son told his friend that he knew precisely what to do to get his father to that point. One night when the friend slept over, the two boys kept talking after they were supposed to be asleep. After two or three warnings, the father blew his cool and reacted in exactly the manner his son had predicted. The boy had learned his father's behavior well enough to predict the sequence of events and have more control than his father.

In this example, the child determined how far to go by weighing the benefits gained from misbehavior compared to the consequences of such behavior. The young man impressed his friend with his ability to predict his father's behavior.

Just asking a child to wait until both Dad and Mom can discuss the situation before arriving at a disciplinary action will increase the child's anxiety. If Dad has always been the heavy in discipline while Mom has tried to "support" the child, try changing these roles and see how that change disrupts predictability. In Dobson's example, had the father responded in a more creative, less predictable way to his son's behavior, the child probably would have at least hesitated and given thought before risking further misbehavior.

Reversal of Responsibility

Reversal of responsibility places accountability for behavior on the child rather than allowing parents to assume responsibility. Parents sometimes get so upset with a child that they react negatively, in frustration and anger. The child then focuses on the adult's anger rather than why the behavior was wrong.

Parents should be simple and direct when confronting a problem. Directness usually conveys that the problem is the child's responsibility. Parents could address a situation with one of these questions:

> "Who is responsible for your behavior?"
> "Who did it?"
> "How could you have handled the problem differently?"
> "Will you handle it that way next time?"

Children like to focus on the reason for misbehavior as opposed to the responsibility they need to assume for having performed it. Parents need to be alert to excuses or irrelevant issues that change the focus or serve to avoid responsibility.

Natural and Logical Consequences

The essence of natural consequences is to let children learn from experience or nature. For example, a child learns by being stung that bees are dangerous; refusing to eat lunch brings about mid-afternoon hunger pains. Natural consequences, although they are quite effective learning tools, can only go so far! Very few parents would allow a child to learn from experience that running into the middle of a busy intersection is not healthy. Nor would parents allow children to learn about electricity by allowing them to play with or around an electrical outlet. Most parents would try to protect their child from a playmate who would demonstrate the true meaning of "an eye for an eye" in response to aggression.

Logical consequences are similar to natural consequences in that consequences are linked to behavior, most likely through a logical, verbal explanation by a parent. For example, it is quite logical that a child who misuses a pool table (an expensive piece of recreational furniture) not be permitted to use it until he or she can demonstrate the responsibility and maturity necessary to use the equipment appropriately. A child who plays hooky from school should be asked to make up the schoolwork on Saturday morning or after school, not as a punitive measure but as a logical one. Because important learning time was misused, the time must be made up. Special activities or watching television can take place after homework but not before; first things must be first, and homework is more important than free time. Logical consequences are also usually understood in advance by the child (for example, as soon as your homework is done, you can watch television, go out to play, etc.).

Mediation Training

Another important technique that helps children learn through discipline is known as mediation training, which is a way of teaching children self-control.[37] An underlying assumption of mediation training is that a child thinks in at least three ways: (1) with words, (2) with mental images, and (3) with motor movements. A child can learn mediation training through these pathways. However, for most children, the verbal thinking approach seems most economical. Through mediation training, children are taught self-control by helping them think through problems by asking the following four questions:

1. What did you do wrong? (problem identification

2. What happens when you (name of misbehavior) that you don't like? (consequences)

3. What should you have been doing? (alternatives)

4. What happens that you like when you (name of appropriate behavior)? (future planning)

Power Struggles

Avoiding power struggles is such an important principle in parenting, yet so difficult to achieve. Parents should try to teach children rather than make them comply. By inviting a child to participate or help them, parents increase the potential for cooperation on the child's part (for example, "Let's do this," not "You do that." "I'll help you clean up your room," not "Go clean up you room right now, or else."). Many times when a parent says "or else," the child is tempted to find out more about "or else," and it becomes a challenge for further study. Parents should have high expectations for their children, believe in them, and expect them to be great. Expecting greatness rather than obedience can make a world of difference in the response one gets from a child. I've never met a child yet that didn't want to be great, but many have more important things to do than be obedient. A good relationship with a child and support of his or her strengths can go a long way toward avoiding power struggles. Parents must also remember to avoid making threats that cannot be enforced.

Additional Techniques

There are several additional disciplinary techniques worth mentioning. The first of these techniques is *anticipating problems*. Parents can try to foresee a problem before it occurs and plan accordingly in an effort to better manage the problem or prevent it from occurring all together. For example, a family vacation that requires six hours of travel time will most likely result in bored and fidgeting children. A wise parent plans several in-car games, stopping for a snack, or play time at a park.

Hurdle help amounts to giving a child a little "lift" to help him or her feel more like doing something. Parents show interest in their son's or daughter's science projects, perhaps by helping collect a few of the insects they need for a collection. This not only demonstrates their interest in the project but gives the children extra help, which spurs them to get started and to complete the task.

Humor works well to defuse a difficult situation. It is important to laugh with children — not *at* them! Make sure your children know you are laughing with them and at whatever the situation is rather than at them, for the latter is an attack on their self-esteem.

Many times putting things in a *game context* works well, especially with necessary responsibilities that aren't very motivating. For example, "Let's see how fast we can rake up the leaves so we can be finished by the time Mom comes home — then we can all go out for ice cream," or "You take that half while I take this one, and let's see who can finish first for the prize of a milkshake — loser buys the milkshake."

When a kid is down, perhaps after receiving a poor grade on a test or some other disappointment, he or she needs a *boost of affection*. A warm comment, an arm around a shoulder, a good word conveying your pride in your child are all good examples of affection that boosts a child's spirit.

Signaling also works well within a family context. The family can agree on signals that mean certain things and are well understood by all family members (for example, a finger to the lip means things are getting too loud, a wink of an eye means you are proud, etc.). Signaling can be a powerful tool for parents or teachers. I can still remember a signal that my kindergarten teacher used to quiet a noisy room — flipping a light switch on and off.

To confront misbehavior and minimize the potential negative effect of focusing on misbehavior rather than appropriate behavior, parents can adopt a practice known as the *punch and burp* approach. A "punch" is the confrontation for misbehavior while the "burp" is a compliment for a positive behavior or attribute. In practice, parents should never "punch" without also "burping" the child. The following dialogue conveys this approach:

> Lee, I'm really so proud to see you play on your team. You really make me proud of your skills, but more than that, of the way you handle yourself. You really look and act so mature. I sure wish you could do as well in your social skills — you know, the way you treat your sister. You could really help her in many ways, but you often put her down. How can you be so good, mature, and act so grown-up in sports, yet act so childish toward your sister?

Positive Approaches to Discipline

The following 36 positive approaches to discipline are adapted from Saf Lerman's Parent Awareness Training.[38]

1. *State your expectations.* Let children know what you expect. Too often adults assume that a child knows what they want, and the child doesn't. Be direct and clear in letting children know what you expect of them.

2. *Be encouraging.* Use encouraging phrases that show you are confident that children can live up to your expectations. Examples of positive ways to phrase your expectations are: "It would be helpful if..."; "I have confidence that..."; "I expect you to..."; "I know you can..."

3. *Appreciate improvements.* Let children know that you notice and appreciate their efforts when they correct a misbehavior and show they are able to cooperate.

4. Spend a great deal of time *praising, acknowledging,* and *appreciating* a child's desirable behavior. This encourages and reinforces it.

5. Adults can help to change unacceptable behavior by *making environmental changes:*

   - If the children are bored, help them to set up constructive activities.
   - If the environment has become too stimulating and active, redirect the children to a quiet activity.
   - If the children are hungry, feed them; if they're tired, adjust sleep schedules.

6. *Prepare children for changes and transitions.* They will cooperate better if they've had time to adjust. For example, "In ten minutes we'll be leaving for the park, so get your shoes on." "This weekend we are going on a visit. Let's think about what you'll need to take with you."

7. *Consider the effect of any emotional stresses* on the children's behavior, and give them plenty of opportunity to work through their feelings in appropriate ways.

8. *Keep in mind the age and stage capabilities* of children and what they are emotionally ready to handle. Try not to ask too much or too little of a child. Adults often believe young children can handle more than they really can. When there is a recurring conflict over the same situation, it could indicate that a child is not capable of what you are asking. Being familiar with developmental stages can keep your expectations realistic.

9. *Distract.* Don't mention the child's misbehavior, but direct his or her attention elsewhere.

10. *Avoid asking a young child questions that encourage a "no" answer* and a possible attack of rebelliousness. Instead of asking, "Do you want to put your shoes on?" be firm and say, "It's time to get your shoes on now."

11. *Be clear and emphatic* when you need to be. Say,

"You must wear your winter jacket this morning. There is no choice in this matter."

12. *Stay simple.* Don't make a long speech when a stern glance or brief "Cut it out" is all that is needed.

13. *State the limit impersonally.* "Walls are not for writing on" is better than "You may not write on walls." This puts the focus on the rule, not the child.

14. *Offer alternatives.* Children need to know what they can do, not just what they cannot do. For example, "The chair is not for jumping on. You can jump on the floor." "People are not for hitting. Hit this pillow instead."

15. *Bend your rules for special occasions.* For example, if bedtime is usually 8:30 and a special television show is on until later or there are special circumstances, you can extend the bedtime hour.

16. *Give the reasons* for your rules and limits.

17. According to the child and the solution, *it may be necessary to repeat the limit.*

18. *Give children the chance to express their feelings* about a situation before expecting them to try and resolve it.

19. *Allow a child in fantasy what he or she can't be allowed in reality:* "You wish you were grown up

and could go to bed much later, but now it's really your bedtime."

20. *Teach the child to use words* instead of hits, kicks, or bites when angry: "You were angry at Jerry, but he is not for hitting. Use words to tell him you are mad at him."

21. When a child needs a more forceful outlet than words for anger and aggression, *encourage him or her to hit a pillow, and help the child to verbalize angry feelings* while doing so. Work toward physical outlets for anger that do not involve hitting, like jumping rope or tossing a basketball.

22. *Give a warning.* Warn children of the effect their behavior is having upon you: "Right now I am still a pleasant person, but in a few minutes, if this keeps up, you'll have an angry person to deal with."

23. *Tell the child you are angry when you are.* Giving your honest disapproval lets children understand the consequences of their behavior, and they will feel more secure when you respond in an honest way about your feelings.

24. *Use statements that express mutual cooperation.* For example, "If you cooperate and let me finish this report, then I will cooperate with your request for help with your schoolwork."

25. When you are in the middle of an argument you

realize you don't even care about, *erase the scene and start again.* Leave the room, come back, and pretend the conflict never happened.

26. *Offer choices:* "You have a choice. You can play ball outside or stay inside and pick something else to do." Choices should be clear-cut, and the parent must be prepared to follow through. If the child remains indoors and continues to throw the ball, the parent needs to take the ball away, saying, "You decided to stay inside; go do something else." Choices help children become more responsible for their actions.

27. *Tell children how their behavior is affecting you,* and then leave them to think of a way to remedy the situation on their own. Instead of saying, "Please turn down the radio so I can hear," a parent could say, "I can't hear on the telephone with the radio so loud" and allow the child to figure out what needs to be done, whether it's closing doors, turning down the volume, or taking the radio to another room.

28. *Whenever feasible, give children some control.* As children get older, they need some flexibility: "You can do your homework whenever you want to, as long as it's done before you watch television."

29. *Begin your request with as soon as.* "As soon as you put your toys away, you can watch television." or "As soon as you brush your teeth, I'll read you a story."

30. *Use role reversal,* in which adult and child pretend to be each other. You can reverse roles just for the fun of it at times and also in discipline situations. Children feel powerful playing the adult role, and then return to being the child refreshed. (Never force a child to reverse roles; only do this if he or she is willing.) A child can play the adult for a short time without being on the spot. This gives the child a few extra moments to think the issue through. By playing the adult a child gets to set his or her own limit and will often pay more attention to it when it is self-formulated. Switching roles lightens the tone, too. Even very young children can appreciate the humor of an adult pretending to be a "tantrumming" child.

31. *Be humorous.* Humor can be a great aid in solving conflicts, whenever you are up to it. Children of all ages appreciate humor at their level.

32. *Use a game-like approach* to enliven routine tasks. Get ideas from television game shows like *Beat the Clock* or use games of chance; for example, everyone who is up, dressed, and completes his or her chores by a certain time gets to draw a number for a lottery.

33. *Put some requests in writing.* When children begin to read, occassionally having a reguest in writing can make it easier to accept: "Dear Jason, You said your clothes would be left in the hamper, not on the floor. How about it? DAD" The child can be encouraged to write back.

34. *Make a deal!* "You can stay up until nine o'clock if you play quietly in your room while we have dinner with our company. Otherwise, You'll need to go to bed at your regular time. Is it a deal?

35. *From time to time, bribe.* Occassionally, it is a reasonable way of making the situation easier for ourselves: "If you are pleasant and cooperative while I go to the supermarket, I'll buy you an ice cream after" or "If you go to bed on time tonight so I can enjoy my company, you'll find a surprise in your shoe tomorrow."

36. *Approach issues as problems to solve.* Adults can encourage children to think of ways to solve a problem, and often the children will come up with excellent, original solutions. If not, the adults can offer positive solutions themselves and include the children in the process of deciding from among them. It's good to agree on a solution acceptable to all. Adults can rely on this approach more and more as children grow older. it's much easier for children to comply with a decision if they helped to make it and their needs were genuinely respected in the process.

VIII

STICKING TO THE ESSENTIALS

Fathers [and mothers], do not exasperate your
children; instead, bring them up in the training and
instruction of the Lord.
Ephesians 6:4

All the essential issues of parenting have never been covered in any single volume, and this book is not an attempt to achieve that nearly impossible goal. However, this chapter is a collection of essentials for Christian parenting that will provide additional insight regarding parenting tasks.

Delight in Your Children

"Delighting" simply means accepting one's children as they are, spontaneously expressing affection for who they are and not what they have accomplished. Children need plenty of free hugs and attention from their parents. Thomas Mullins, a Quaker minister who authored *When 2 or 3 Are Gathered Together Someone Spills his Milk,* says that parents can learn to love their children despite spilled milk. Our children can at times make us so proud that loving them is easy. It is the times when their angelic qualities disappear that delighting in them becomes more of a challenge. Those uninhibited youngsters who tell all the family secrets that were never intended to go beyond the door of our home (let alone to the backyard, the neighborhood, the school, the church, or the in-laws) make delighting quite difficult. Regardless of trying situations, delighting must be a part of every parent-child relationship.

As parents, we must not forget to enjoy our children even in those trying moments. If we only pause for a moment, laugh with our kids, and have some fun with them, we would discover how wonderfully made they really are. By taking notice of our children, we prepare ourselves to handle even the largest challenge that might try our patience. Delighting helps parents look at problems as opportunities.

Because we live in such a fast-paced society, it is easy to miss important moments that can help us and our children to grow. Lest we are too busy, let us make planned and concerted efforts to take notice of our children. Although psychological research confirms that parental warmth is associated positively with the child developing high self-esteem, many parents spend only a few minutes per day in childcare functions. Self-worth is one of the most important elements of our children's emotional health, and delighting in them is a good way to build their esteem and confidence.

Sticking to the Essentials

Respect Your Children

People should be respected, and children are people, too! Parents and other adults should treat children with much care, not misleading or discouraging them in any way. Adults often do things to children that they would never do to another adult. Adults often ignore, belittle, or criticize children needlessly and usually without regard for their feelings. Those same adults would not attempt to administer such treatment to one of their peers, but children are expected to grin and bear it.

I have often seen parents make feeble attempts at disciplining their children in public by ridiculing them in front of peers or other people. Such poor parenting is usually ineffective as discipline but is doubly destructive to children's self-worth. In such situations, a child often tries to save face with peers or defend his or her ego by openly challenging the parent, which results in a power struggle where neither parent nor child wins.

Parents should always discipline in private if possible. I don't buy the excuse some parents use that if children misbehave in public they deserve to be disciplined in public. In such situations, one needs to examine the motivation behind the discipline. Is the goal for the child to internalize a value to apply in future situations or is it for all to see that the parent is a good parent who disciplines his or her children? Still worse, is the discipline given in anger by a parent who feels better after confronting the child? Public discipline of a child does not lead to admiration. I've often wanted to give those parents my business card and suggest private therapy.

Several years ago, I attended an evangelistic crusade in Columbus, Ohio. While waiting for the service to start one evening, I amused myself by observing the people sitting around me. I was enjoying watching a toddler make his way from a row of seats down to the front of the auditorium. I was further amused that his parents, who were socializing with friends, had not noticed his departure. After discovering that the child was missing and being chagrined at his whereabouts, the embarrassed father made his way down to the front of the auditorium, picked the little guy up and raised him above his head to swat him on the rump three or four times. My amusement quickly changed to anger. I'm sure the real goal behind such a display was to make Dad feel less embarrassed rather than to have the toddler internalize the value of staying in his seat while attending crusades.

Admit Errors and Ask Forgiveness When Wrong

Some parents act as though they never err; others are too proud or ashamed to admit they make errors. Still other parents admit error to peers but never to their children. Admitting to others when one is wrong is not a sign of weakness but of strength. None of us are perfect, but only some of us are honest and mature enough to admit our faults. Recognizing errors and admitting responsibility takes courage; however, it is the first step toward remediating the mistake.

When parents admit mistakes to their children, they are modeling humanity and humility — both good qualities to teach children. By asking forgiveness, parents model not only that they are human and sometimes make errors, but that they are honest in accepting responsibility for changing wrongs. In many respects, a parent's error can be a golden opportunity to model and teach significant values in positive interpersonal relationships. There is nothing more healing for a family than the act of asking a loved one's forgiveness. Asking a child to forgive us can be the start for rebuilding a positive and loving parent-child relationship.

Give Children Opportunities to Provide Input and Help Make Decisions

Parents should encourage their children to take an active part in the family by allowing them to provide input regarding family decisions. Psychological research reports that children with high self-esteem often come from homes that are democratic, with every member of the family participating. Of course, parents must retain their God-given responsibility to oversee the family, asking for input on appropriate issues and making judicious use of suggestions.

However, if parents practice this principle and look for opportunities where children can have a part in decision making, the children will learn about decision making, cooperation, and the democratic process as well as feel involved. Most adults would refuse to participate on a committee or work crew that was run the way some parents run their families. Industries promote *participatory management* — getting input from all who are involved and letting them participate in decision making. Such a process usually yields much better output; most people find it easier to support something they have helped to create. Families that are more participatory will probably have fewer heartaches to endure!

Parents should look for opportunities to elicit involvement of the children, for example, vacations and weekend events. Children should be kept abreast of family finances and situations that limit the range of such activities, such as a pay cut or the loss of a job or mom's pregnancy.

Build Family Traditions

Edith Schaeffer talks about building a "museum of memories," the traditions that are remembered by children long after they have left home and that they will probably practice in their own families. Traditions include the manner in which we celebrate birthdays, whether we open gifts on Christmas Eve or Christmas Day, and special events in the family's life. The value we place on little league baseball games, hiking through the park, saying or singing grace at the dinner table, or riding bikes on Sunday afternoon will determine whether such activities become family traditions. Primary among family traditions are establishing a family altar and prayer times.

I have found that it is not necessarily the expensive activities that are remembered by children. Even though trips to a rather expensive amusement park will be cherished by all members of the family, creative, inexpensive activities can have equal value if done in a manner that makes them memorable. The important element isn't the money spent but the fellowship that family members share which makes an event significant to each member. Riding bikes, flying kites, walking through the park, or just taking a drive to the Dairy Queen after yard work on a hot Saturday afternoon can achieve this goal without taxing the family budget. Family activities become traditions precisely because they have meaning and value to family members.

Other family traditions we practice combine necessary household duties with play and fellowship. For example, my son and I have always mowed the grass together. As a young child, his involvement was quite limited and lengthened rather than shortened the time required for the task. Many times, he would ride in the wheel barrow on the way back from dumping grass trimmings or be pulled in his wagon while mowing. As he matured, however, he was able to take on more responsibility and later assumed the bulk of this task with some assistance from his father.

Prioritizing such practices not only legitimizes the family and the importance of each member but marks the importance of establishing family memories. Traditions help us remember significant events and values, and gives meaning to parents' teaching. Our memories of the family help us prioritize the values of the family as well as keep those priorities straight as we complete necessary responsibilities. In a day when the significance of the family is diminishing rapidly, it is crucial that Christian parents preserve its significance.

Spend Time with Your Children

Some parents try to fulfill their role in the most efficient way they can — doing as little as possible or contracting the function out to others. This is not to criticize the use of day-care centers, preschools, or babysitters, for they are necessary when both parents work. But parents must take sufficient time to perform the tasks related to the role of parenting. Quality time is more important than quantity, but the tasks of parenting *do* take time, and responsibilities must be prioritized in a way that allows parents to take that time.

Quality time is giving a youngster undivided attention. It conveys to the child that he or she is a most important person and that the parent cares and is concerned about the child's interests. In many cases, if a child feels that he or she has a parent's undivided attention for a few minutes that child will be satisfied and allow the parent to return to reading the paper or watching the evening news. However, most parents try to minister to their children's needs while doing something else as well. Usually the child recognizes that the news has higher priority than a game or tea party. Even though a parent may have spent a reasonable quantity of time with a child, the value is limited if the child had to compete with something else. Some parents tell me that they spend enormous amounts of time with their children and in desperation say, "It seems like the more time I spend with Sarah, the more she demands of me — she just never gets enough attention." These parents may be giving quantity time rather than quality time. Try joining your children for Saturday morning cartoons for an hour or so; you might be surprised at how enjoyable such an activity can be. You will probably be given the remaining morning hours to accomplish necessary tasks.

Listen, Listen, Listen, and Listen!

There is probably no more important element in communication than listening, for true communication involves more listening than talking. Parents need to remember that communication includes both verbal and nonverbal behaviors. It is very frustrating and aggravating for parents to talk to a child who is nonverbally not giving them the time of day. If it is the parent who is merely going through the motions of listening, the child may become frustrated with and angry at the parent. About 70% to 80% of our communication is nonverbal and only about 20% to30% is verbal. So rather than just telling a child we are interested in listening, we must act like we are.

Children often get the impression that what they have to say is unimportant because adults seem to ignore them or disregard their conversations or questions, and they feel that they are to be seen and not heard. I'm not implying that children should be made a part of every adult conversation; however, if children feel a part of discussions where appropriate, they may exhibit fewer attention-getting behaviors that interfere with adult conversations.

Parents might get to know their children better if they listen to them. If parents stop long enough to listen to what their children are saying to them and each other, they truly know them; and by knowing their children, parents better understand them. By better understanding them, they are more capable of establishing a better relationship with them!

Avoid Power Struggles and Be Fair

Parents should save their threats. Generally, parents regret having made them and usually make them at a time when they are angry. Many threats are impossible to carry out. Quite often, parents will say they're going to do things that they really can't do, should not do, or do not even wish to do. More importantly, threats move us from a position of relationships and power to one of no choice and generally right smack dab into a power struggle, where the youngster has far more of the share of power. After all, the child can always act "childish," but the adult is not permitted to act immature or irresponsible.

Power struggles quite often encourage the child to obey maliciously or "smart off," but still be doing what was asked of him. Dobson, in a film series titled *Turn Your Heart Toward Home* , tells a story about a family on a vacation trip. The two children start the trip with great expectations: however, as the trip progresses, they become bored and start acting up and disregard warnings from their father. Finally, in desperation, the father stops the car, takes both children out of the car and spanks them, telling them he doesn't want to hear a word out of them for the next two hours. After two hours, the little boy gracefully asks his father, "Is it okay to talk now?" Once granted permission by his father, the young lad says, "When you spanked me back there two hours ago, I lost my shoe as you put me back in the car.

You told me I couldn't say anything, so I didn't." This is a good example of malicious obedience.

Parents need to be fair. If we didn't see what happened, we should not make assumptions just because it has happened this way several times before. If this is the exception to the pattern, blaming the child may be the devastation we will never live down or undo. Parents also need to focus on the positive rather than the negative. Parents violate this rule by ignoring their youngsters until they misbehave, thus focusing all their attention on incorrect or negative behavior. Too often, parents utilize such negative statements of control such as "take your feet off that chair" when they could respond in a more positive manner without decreasing any of the assertiveness the response carries. For example, an alternative to such a statement could be "please place your feet on the floor, where they belong." Other examples include "please place your coat in the proper place" rather than "get your coat off the floor — you don't live in a barn."

Model Christ

Christ taught the majority of his lessons by example. The importance of modeling has already been emphasized. Parents should model the life we hope our children will learn to live. Parents modeling values, morals, beliefs will go much further in helping their children identify and internalize these more than any hard-sell lectures or other forms of coercion. If parents model Christ in their everyday living, they will be impressed with the impact it has upon their children's behavior.

127

IX

Remaining Patient During Adolescence

But the fruit of the Spirit is love, joy, peace,
patience, kindness, goodness, faithfulness,
gentleness, and self control. Against such things
there is no law.
Galatians 5:22

No publication on parenting would be complete without spending some time on the period of adolescence, for it is thought to be the most difficult period of all parenting. Some parents are victorious as "good parents" until their children become teenagers, and then it seems as if something radically changes, for they lose their confidence and creativity. After losing confidence in themselves, they seem to accept this developmental period as totally unmanageable. Some parents in desperation disown their children, while others continue to claim them as part of the family but describe them to others as an entity totally beyond reason or understanding.

Regardless of how parents feel about this period of development, it can be challenging to even the best of us. It is a time that taxes our many resources as we attempt to help our children mature in a stormy period. Some parents get far more concerned than they need to, for they fret and plan for the worst — setting up expectations that their children will be totally unreasonable. Since they expect negative behavior, their children live up to their expectations. All stages of child development have both their challenges and rewards. Adolescence is no different than other stages in this regard, only publicized more. Adults must deal with the changes they must go through during their life cycle. Adapting to change isn't merely an adolescent phenomenon.

Adolescence is by definition a transitional stage, a time when one is no longer a child, yet still not an adult. Teens feel and certainly experience that they are "in between" or in a transition. Any life transition can be difficult, let alone one with as many aspects as adolescence. Not only do teens get the perception from others that they are in an in-between stage, but they probably also feel quite ambivalent about which way to go. Since adolescence for most children starts at about twelve or thirteen years of age, a child must begin accomplishing this transition into adulthood with very little experience.

Rather than being helpful to teens, adults seem to increase stress by frequently telling them to "grow up," "be more mature," or "stop acting like a child." However, the moment a young man or woman tries to do this, the adults send inconsistent messages, which add to young people's confusion. "You're really not old enough to do this." When you get older you can take on this responsibility." "Now that you're a teenager, you think you know everything about life." These inconsistent messages cause teens to feel misunderstood and that only peers, who may be experiencing similar transitional issues, understand them. As young people turn to their friends in desperation and begin to exchange views, they receive understanding, which then strengthens the peer relationship and reinforces a declining respect for parents or adults who don't seem to understand.

In addition to being in a state of transition with expectations and roles being redefined, the young person experiences physical, cognitive, and emotional changes — all interacting with each other. Physical changes become quite obvious as puberty begins. Not only does the body start changing in appearance but the chemical and hormonal balance shifts to one of extreme activity with hormonal drives during adolescence. These hormonal changes can cause the adolescent to react more emotionally than in prior stages with reactive, angry outbursts, depressive episodes, increased anxiety and insecurity. Emotional extremes are more likely during this period of development. Adolescents begin to think like adults and become much more of a challenge to the adults around them. They can go beyond the concrete or simplistic thinking characteristic of early childhood and can now think more like adults. For the first time in a young person's life, he or she becomes concerned about the hypothetical, the future, the remote. Unlike earlier childhood when the parents' word was generally taken as final, the teenager starts to challenge parents' rationale and questions their reasoning.

Emotionally, adolescents go through many changes as well. Young people begin thinking of themselves as individuals, apart from parents, and they strive for emancipation or autonomy. As teens strive to pull away from parents, they become preoccupied with acceptance by their social group or peers. Peer influence becomes more important than family.

Although desiring the emotional security and acceptance from parents, most adolescent energies are directed toward the peer group as they worry about physical appearance, attractiveness, and physical development. The teen's values take on a similarity to those of the peer group as opposed to teachings from family and upbringing. This, of course, further worries parents, who have for the first several years of the child's life tried to teach appropriate values that now seem disregarded.

All these changes are quite challenging to parents who have remained the most significant people in their child's life until now. All of a sudden, a father is discounted as someone who doesn't quite know the way things are in the modern world. Mothers, likewise, have a difficult time understanding their children as they try to be supportive and are pushed away. Power struggles begin, especially when the parent refuses to change the normal way of doing things.

Sometimes a rift occurs in the parent-child relationship, which has for years been called the generation gap. There does not need to be a generational gap between parent and child. However, communication must be kept open and practiced from a very young age if parents wish to have their children enter into adolescence and continue open communication with them. Unfortunately, habits and patterns are hard to change, and usually a poor pattern of communication in early parent-child relationships does not alter itself when the child becomes a teenager. By the time a child enters adolescence, if no one has been truly listening, the child recognizes that and eliminates any efforts. Parents then get overly concerned because their teenagers are secretive, isolated, noncommunicative, and share more with friends than family.

Despite the difficulties adolescence brings for parents, they must cautiously avoid pushing the teenager over the edge! Dobson in "Focus on the Family" seminars encourages parents to prepare themselves for helping their children through adolescence by taking every opportunity to tolerate and support them. Parents can take their cue from Scripture: Right now it is not pleasant to deal with this problem, yet I know that if my child can gain insight and be more adequately trained through it, this situation will bear fruit in the days ahead (see Hebrews 12:11).

Parents must accept the fact that adolescents rebel! The rebellion does not have to be aggressive in nature and tends not to be so if parents have accepted this phenomenon of adolescence as a natural phase of development. By better preparation on the parent's part, this period of development can be tolerated and lived through by both parents and children as adolescents strive to become independently functioning people who think for themselves. Perhaps parents need to stop trying to force children through development during this period but begin to show acceptance and cooperation.

The following simple illustration [39] depicts the importance of cooperation as two people strive for their goals. Some parents and their adolescents never get beyond the third or fourth levels. The first two levels seem to illustrate the power struggles characteristic in many homes with adolescents. The third and fourth levels appear to represent the generation gap many parents feel with their adolescents. Levels five and six represent the cooperation and understanding that will assist the young person's transition into adulthood.

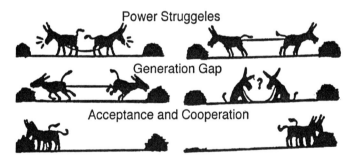

Power Struggeles

Generation Gap

Acceptance and Cooperation

Starting good parenting practices when a child becomes a teenager may be too late. The ideal parent will start effective parenting practices when the child is brought home from the hospital and even begin thinking about parenting strategies during pregnancy. However, if this has not happened, there are a few suggestions that might help during this time.

First, parents should *prepare themselves for adolescence by working out their own attitude*. Many a parent criticizes their children during adolescence for constantly showing a poor attitude about things, yet they never stop to look at their own, which in many cases is a poor model for their children — often an adult version of what they see and criticize in their son or daughter. Parents must begin thinking differently by trying to expand their level of tolerance during this period of development. Helping a child through adolescence can be an exciting challenge.

I can remember one of my more challenging times as a parent to be that of potty training my son. I became quite frustrated in that my psychology training and techniques did not work. The harder I tried, the more frustrated I got! After giving up in frustration and saying that perhaps we had started this process before our son was indeed ready for this teaching, he accomplished on his own what I could not teach him with all my expertise gained from having completed a master's degree in psychology and devoting one entire Saturday to this task. I'm not saying that potty training is more difficult than entering into adolescence but that challenges face us throughout life. Such challenges might range from potty training a toddler to school adjustment problems during elementary school, and from autonomy seeking in adolescence to caring for an aged parent in later life. No one period of time need be given credit as the "worst" or most difficult. Accepting this concept might help to improve our attitude about adolescence.

A parent's attitude is most important! Parents who

expect the worst will quite often get the worst. Parents need to be optimistic that they and their children will make it. We probably should just relax and not become reactionary, for we lose creativity and the ability to be spontaneous when under stress.

Second, parents must be willing to *accept emancipation or independence striving as normal.* Parents certainly want their children to become independent and capable of moving out on their own, holding a responsible job, making responsible decisions, and being respectable law-abiding citizens. Adolescence is a time for sons and daughters to learn these very important skills. Perhaps the many opportunities this period affords a young person will not always turn out to be successful, but parents must not forget they themselves have learned from mistakes. Some of us continue to learn the most important lessons in life from failure. Parents should look for opportunities for teens to give their opinions and make up their own minds. This task is difficult for parents because they have been making decisions for their children in an effort to protect them and have likewise always been there to rescue them. I admit to helping my son on several homework projects, which enabled him ("us") get a better grade. Perhaps, my help would have been needed less if I had been more willing to allow him to suffer once or twice when his lack of planning caused the natural consequence of failure. As a concerned parent, I would have still been there to help when he asked for it, but my "rescue tendencies" would not have given him the easy out and thus kept him from learning from his mistakes.

Third, parents need to *demonstrate a positive*

outlook or optimism. Parents would do better if they learned to ignore some things. Parents must guard against exaggerating the difficulties they face on the home front. I get angry when I hear some parents talk about the misery they are experiencing because of their teenagers. From their descriptions, one would swear they were talking about beasts of the lowest form — not God's creations and products of their parental teaching and upbringing. If parents adopt the philosophy that problems are opportunities, this period of development will go much smoother than if they choose to harp on every challenge or disagreement they have with their sons or daughters.

Fourth, parents must *begin communication with their children.* One hopes that parents would have established some good communication patterns, but if not, they must begin. It is never too late to change! In a news story printed in *The Columbus Dispatch,* Julia Osborne summarized what several professionals working with adolescents prioritized for communicating with them. Parents are encouraged to:[40]

1) *Listen* but not tell them how to deal with things.

2) *Talk* to them on their time, not only when it's convenient for the parent.

3) Talk to them *privately.*

4) *Watch their tone of voice* and body language.

5) *Acknowledge their child's feelings* by showing respect for attitudes.

6) *Express feelings* about their behavior without attacking it or them.

7) *Ask for explanations,* or what happened rather than why.

8) *Ask* for more details.

9) *Avoid telling* too many anecdotes.

10) *Pick their battles,* but be willing to compromise when appropriate.

11) *Avoid using absolutes.*

12) *Work on solving problems* together.

13) *Remember* that their children are growing up.

14) *Provide positive, constructive comments* when possible.

15) *Coordinate a united front* as parents by being consistent.

16) *Be patient* and "hang in there."

17) *Seek advice* when necessary.

Fifth (and closely associated with the fourth), parents should *focus on the relationship and strive to be a good friend* by taking on the characteristics of a friend. A friend does not condemn, criticize, or ostracize. A friend cautions when someone is headed toward danger but in a caring, supportive manner that makes the message more acceptable. A friend likewise takes an interest in the things that are important to that individual. A friend gives the gift of understanding and is slow to judge.[41] Being a friend takes time. I might not be at all interested in Saturday afternoon wrestling, but I can enhance my father-son relationship immensely if I take the time to view it with my son. I may not understand the latest fashion in dress, hairstyles, and totally lack appreciation for contemporary music, but I can work on accepting the importance it may have for my daughter if I am to become her true friend. At least I can try to understand it by showing some effort and some respect for my children's opinions.

Last, and perhaps most important of all, *parents must model what they would like to see* in their teen's behavior. "Actions speak louder than words" is just not an old cliché but is a practice that works quite well. This practice works well in all levels of childhood but perhaps best during adolescence. During this period of parenting, the parents' influence is almost nil compared to all the other forces that compete for the teenager's attention and focus. If teenagers will not listen to their parents, at least their parents can show them through their modeling what they would like to see them grow up to be. The majority of studies in human development confirm that adolescents tend to reclaim the value system of their parents after they get through this period of questioning and sometimes rebelliousness. Most parents would be better off if they talked less and acted more. This is why Dobson refers to more things being caught than taught all through childhood.

An article once appeared in *Possibilities* by Robert Schuller Ministries that focused on teenage rebellion and alcoholism. A follow-up to this article focused on parent-teenager communication. This excerpt ends by exhorting the parent as well as the teenager to be patient and pray. What better way to close this chapter?[42]

How to Talk to Your Teen

Put Yourself in Their Shoes. Do you remember how you felt when you were thirteen, fifteen, seventeen? If you were like most teenagers, you probably worried excessively about what your peers thought of you. Sometimes you felt awkward and unattractive. You fluctuated between feeling grown up and hopelessly childish. But you survived, and your teens will, too. By remembering what it was like, you can be a more understanding parent.

Listen. The majority of teens complain that parents do not really hear them when they speak. Active listening allows you to focus on the other person's feelings and send back a message of empathetic understanding. You do not need to evaluate, offer advice, analyze, or ask a lot of questions. Understand their true concerns first before responding.

Use Words That Build Up, Not Tear Down. Your teen needs your encouragement more than you might think. Discouraging words such as "You never do it right!" or "You're always late!" tend to kill self-esteem. If a conversation starts to heat up, take a time out before sarcastic, cutting words slip out.

Be Honest. Let your teen see you as the imperfect, but growing, human that you are. You do not have to have all the answers to maintain their respect. Share with them how you worry about being a good parent and sometimes do not know how to handle the problems that come up. Most important, admit when you have been wrong.

Be Patient and Pray. Remember, God knows what it's like to be a parent. He wants the best for you and your teen. Talk to God often about your concerns and encourage your teen to do likewise. Allow God to become an invisible, loving member of your family.

How to Talk to Your Parents

Put Yourself in Their Shoes. They may not want to admit it, but your parents sometimes feel inadequate as leaders in your family. It is especially unnerving for them to see their "little" boy or girl suddenly growing up. They worry that they have not done enough to teach good values. Understanding how your parents feel may help you be more sensitive to their concerns.

Try Not to Retreat. Many parents complain that their teenagers never talk to them anymore. The closeness they once experienced is replaced with stony silences. Often they do not understand your need for privacy and independence, or how it hurts you when they pretend to hear you but are not really listening. Tell your parents the kind of things that make you want to clam up. And listen to their concerns, too.

Use Words that Communicate Respect. If you are like most teens, you do not like some of the restrictions your parents have placed upon you. You may not understand their reasons for the rules. Try to talk openly and calmly with your parents about what bothers you. Use "I" messages: "I know that this is important to you, but it makes me feel you do not trust me. Help me understand your reasoning." If a conversation begins to deteriorate into an angry exchange, take a time out and resume the talk later. Or write out your feelings.

Be Honest. It is difficult to tell the whole truth if you are worried about your parents' reactions. But remember that they were your age once, too, and probably understand your problems better than you think. Give them a chance to help you by keeping the communication lines open.

Be Patient and Pray. God is not finished with you — or your parents — yet! All of you have more growing to do. Allow God to be your heavenly parent, the one you turn to for guidance on how you relate to your earthly parents.

X

APPROACHING SPECIAL CHALLENGES

When pride comes, then comes disgrace, but with
humility comes wisdom.
Proverbs 11:2

Although the concepts presented in this book apply to all parenting situations, there are many factors that can disrupt the usual course of parenting, requiring unique skills and expanded understanding to meet the challenge. While divorce will severely impact many homes and the parenting styles, there are many other factors that can cause disruption in the course of parenting. Some homes with both parents present can be as dysfunctional as ones resulting from divorce or some other major trauma in the lives of children. Christians are not exempt from problems; all too often families within the church will be faced with challenging stressors. Divorce or premature death of a spouse sometimes leaves one parent to raise children; if single parents choose to remarry, they are faced with the challenge of reconstituting the family, and the role of step-parenting comes into play. Christian couples who are not able to have children of their own or who wish to open their homes and hearts to a needy child are choosing to become adoptive parents. Although adoption of an infant child may not pose any greater challenge than having natural children, many adoptions involve children beyond infancy and ones that have multiple needs. Foster parenting a needy child on a temporary basis is a special ministry for families that have the resources and the commitment required to handle such situations successfully. As the number of children needing foster care surges, the pool of good homes available appears inadequate to meet the demand. What a beautiful opportunity this ministry is!

To understand the implications of such specialized parental roles, let us first turn our attention to some of the characteristics that cause dysfunction within the family unit. According to Peter Gerlock, there are several characteristics that seem to prevail in dysfunctional families.[43] This does not imply that all such features will be present in any home experiencing trouble, but such features may be present to one degree or another.

Dysfunctional families seem to reproduce themselves. Poor habits, attitudes, and teaching that prevail in such families usually have a history going back to previous generations, and these "customs" seem to be inherited from one generation to the next.

Although help is available to these families, they tend to be closed to resources or ideas outside the family.

Family secrets often exist, but they are well-defended through denial the and projection of blame onto others outside the family, including institutions such as church, school, and community agencies or other family-related organizations. Such secrets can range from unfaithfulness of the parents to drug abuse and alcoholism. Other family secrets may include physical or sexual abuse of one or more of its members or some other acting out behavior that is well hidden by the family.

Although members of all families have some degree of emotional expression, dysfunctional family members often exhibit greater emotional expression than those from nondysfunctional families. They may experience an excess of certain emotions such as fear, shame, and guilt. Inconsistent humor — too little humor or hurtful forms of humor — can be characteristic in these families. Frequently such families have rigid or inconsistent rules. Role reversal between members of the family, especially in the parent-child roles, is common. This phenomenon can include grandparents if the extended family members are an active part of the dysfunction within the family. Instead of buffer to protect children from outside stressors, parents become stressors to their children. Instead of teaching, protecting, modeling, and encouraging growth in a positive manner, parents give messages to their offspring that convey rejection and neglect in meeting the child's needs and fulfilling the parental role.

The list of parental messages in dysfunctional

homes, either stated or perceived, often includes the following: "Don't trust." "Don't talk." "I love you, but go away." "You're wonderful. You're worthless." "You're responsible for our family problems." "I'll love you if... ." Such messages leave children to internalize blame for their family's dysfunction and unhappiness. As a result of such messages, children experience shame, guilt, hurt, and anger. The message that "feelings are not okay" seems to predominate at all levels in the dysfunctional family. Physical, emotional, and sexual abuse are often associated with such homes. The dynamics of such families vacillate between the extremes of *enmeshment,* where all members are too closely entangled with each other without sufficient boundaries, to the opposite extreme of *disengagement,* where all members of the family operate independently and show no investment in or support of each other.

With divorce, children experience what Judith Wallerstein describes as an extended period of disequilibrium, which may last several years or longer.[44] Based on a ten-year study of divorcing families, Wallerstein reports that the adjustments required for the child following a divorce or bereavement in losing a parent will stretch over several years of childhood and adolescence. According to this research, which is highly regarded within the child development field, the child will need to accomplish six major tasks to successfully survive the effects of such a loss.

The first task is to *acknowledge the reality of the marital rupture.* Most children, like adults, tend to deny that the family unit they have known is disrupting or changing. Such change is usually not desired by children, nor have they had any input, making acceptance a bigger challenge. Most children of divorce continue for years to have the fantasy that their birth parents will get back together and that all of them can live happily ever after. This fantasy, along with fears of parental abandonment, disaster, being overwhelmed by feelings of sorrow, anger, and rejection, and a yearning for keeping things the way they were further hamper the task of acknowledgment. Much like a child who has lost a parent from death, the child of divorce fears losing the other parent and being left alone; that fear is so strong that it may keep the child from resolving this task for some time. Through adult support and mutual parenting of the child by both parents, the child can master this task in about one year from the separation.

The second major task for the child of divorced parents is what Wallerstein calls *disengaging from parental conflict and distress and resuming customary pursuits* (school and play, relationships), which can take up to one-and-a-half years following the separation. As difficult as it may seem for parents who are still very angry at each other for the things that may have caused the divorce, they need to help their children see their difficulties as a parental issue and not allow children to personalize blame. Quite often parents continue to keep their children in the middle of the conflict rather than allowing them to deal with their own feelings about the trauma they have experienced. Once children are given opportunities to acknowledge and handle their own feelings of anxiety, depression, and loss, they can resolve such feelings and turn attention back to school peer relationships and other normal childhood issues.

Divorced parents may not have anything in common except their children, but it is most important that they communicate and provide some consistency in conveying their continued love and support for the children. Instead of spousal parents who are married, they may need to become "professional" parents who are no longer in love or married. Parenting may need to take on the context of a job with a cooperative attitude and respect between co-workers. People can learn to work with someone they don't love. Out of respect for each other as persons, they learn to cooperate as co-workers and produce a common product or work toward the same goal. In the case of divorced parents, the product is their children and the goal is helping them attain adulthood successfully.

The third task children of divorce must accomplish has to do with *resolving the loss* children feel in the disruption of their family. According to Wallerstein's research, this task may be one of the most difficult ones, and it may take several years to establish a good relationship with a future step-parent. Children must overcome a sense of rejection, lovelessness, powerlessness, responsibility or blame for the loss of family, and other such self-defeating feelings. This task is accomplished by establishing a reliable visiting pattern and ongoing communication with the parent with whom the child no longer lives. Continually reminding the child of his or her parents' love and the child's blamelessness in the divorce is an absolute must to reassure the child and help reach resolution of this task. Family therapy sessions including both birth parents and step-parents are often necessary during this stage to assist the family in giving the child this message and to work out consistent visiting plans and other such arrangements.

Resolving anger and self-blame is the fourth major task for children of divorce. Children generally always seem to blame someone — either mother, father, or more than likely in divorce situations, themselves. Quite often after blame surfaces, anger follows. In some situations, anger can be long-standing and intense, especially among older children and adolescents. The goal of this task is to assist children in achieving some perspective regarding the reasons that prompted the divorce as well as understanding that both parents continue to care for and love them as they always did. As with the third task, ongoing reassurance regarding the child's lack of blame or guilt in the divorce and redefining it as an adult issue that really had nothing to do with the children may be helpful. Depending on the level of conflict and maturity of the family members attempting to accomplish this task, this task can take as long as five to ten years to accomplish successfully and may require outside professional help in therapy.

Fifth, the child must accept the *permanence or finality of divorce*. Such acceptance may take the child years to accept, even when a parent remarries. Lastly, Wallerstein says a child will need to achieve *realistic hope regarding relationships*. Having survived the loss of a desirable relationship or having been challenged to accept redefinitions of their families as a result of the divorce, children will need to resolve their feelings regarding it to have optimism regarding their future relationships, especially as adults. Continued focus on children's needs and interests by both parents as well as reassurance of their love can be a great asset in helping children through these last two tasks successfully.

There are a multitude of other issues for children who experience divorce and will for at least part of their childhood live in a single-parent home. Peter Gerlock says that such children encounter many changes in their lives.[45] They will need to survive the disbelief, shock, guilt, self-doubt, fear, hurt, rage, blame, shame, and depression that often follows the announcement of divorce or separation by their parents. Following such a shock comes the reality of having less time with parents and being alone more. Not only will they see the noncustodial parent less, but they will also see less of the custodial parent as he or she performs additional tasks in the absence of the other parent.

Children are quite often given parental status, which Gerlock calls *parentification* in hopes that they will take on more responsibility.[46] This is certainly not conducive to helping the child deal with the divorce. Some single parents even try putting their adolescent or preadolescent sons or daughters in a more adult role in an effort to encourage more independence and responsibility. In addition to all these changes in the young person's life, he or she is also faced with a redefinition of roles and rules with grandparents, siblings, and peers. Do the children continue to have the same kind of relationship with grandparents and see them as frequently as they did prior to the divorce? Are visits to the noncustodial grandparents cut off? Do older children have to take on babysitting roles for younger children in the family, severely limiting their ability to participate in peer, social, or school activities? All these and other questions are ones that face children and families experiencing divorce.

Divorce often disrupts the physical environment; larger homes must be sold to meet a reduced budget and family size. Such changes can also cause changes in school placement, which may have adverse effects on children's motivation and performance. Amid all these changes, children probably fear further loss; prior security is lost to feelings of hopelessness and powerlessness about what is happening in their lives. Although very important to helping children get through the trauma of divorce successfully, grieving is often postponed or put off in hopes that their dreams of parental reconciliation will somehow come true.

If children are successful in getting through the various tasks related to divorce, chances are good that their lives will change once again because of remarriage. A child has probably just begun feeling less anxious and angry as he or she begins accepting the new situation as "okay" when he or she is once again thrust into the challenge of change. In most cases, the child is challenged to deal with the prospect of a step-parent much too soon after the divorce of his parents and prior to accomplishing the developmental tasks that help resolve the divorce issue for the child.

While trying to "finish up" the divorce, the family takes on a new relationship with a step-parent. Loyalty conflicts surface almost immediately. The children will wonder what to call the new step-parent — by his or her first name, or "Dad" or "Mom." If they refer to the step-parent as dad or mom, does that mean they feel their natural parent is less significant with the step-parent in the picture? There may be a different set of rules and expectations, roles will change, and sometimes the parent pressures children toward complete acceptance of and loyalty to the new step-parent. Other times, the new step-parent, in exuberance, tries to take on too much leadership in the family and especially in discipline of his or her step-children. Most research studies available on step-parenting recommend that the step-parent progress quite slowly in taking an active role in discipline of step-children, leaving the major parental tasks to the natural parent and putting all his or her effort toward building a good relationship with step-children based on love, care, acceptance, and appreciation. Both step-parents and step-children need time to get to know each other and develop this relationship. A step-parent thus faces not only the usual experiences of child rearing but also the child's problems and feelings resulting from a major upset in his life.[47]

As with divorce, there are several developmental tasks that step-children need to go through to deal with changes successfully. First, they must grieve multiple losses. As already mentioned, many children continue to hold onto the fantasy that their divorced parents will get back together, despite indications to the contrary. When one or the other parent remarries, the child comes one step closer toward the realization that such a dream probably will not occur. Upon considering such a reality, the guilt and self-doubt that followed the divorce may resurface and need to be resolved again. While trying once again to resolve the loss involved in the divorce and the accompanying emotions, children must redefine "Who's my family?" Discipline, diet, division of labor, and turf issues all create problems that are not easy, but are nonetheless manageable if family members learn to cooperate.[48]

Foster homes are intended for temporary placement of children who should eventually return to their biological families. Adoption is a permanent commitment to the adoptive child; the rights and responsibilities of the biological parents are terminated and legally transferred to the adoptive parents. Adoption has made marvelously happy family life possible for many childless people, and it may answer questions or doubts some people experience about having children.[49] Foster homes often provide temporary placement for youngsters whose families are in crisis or who need protective services to prevent abuse and neglect.

A great number of children are made available for adoption, either surrendered voluntarily by parents or permanently removed from their homes for their safety and protection because they have been abused or neglected. For children who come from such homes, only specialized environments with available resources and therapies should be considered for placement. Such children have often experienced more than one divorce, several step-parents, and more than one foster or adoptive home placement. Specialized treatment settings designed to help children who suffer such traumas can successfully treat the children and prepare them to return to their families or another family setting — either foster or adoptive homes. For Christian parents who wish to take on this ministry, further training and a greater awareness of related issues will be helpful. Such parenting situations will probably require support from a professional therapist to assist with a child's ongoing adjustment and development.

Epilogue

A Reasonable Challenge

For nothing is impossible with God.
Luke 1:37

I can do everything through him who gives me
strength.
Philippians 4:13

Despite the commitment we have to our children and the challenge that we may feel as Christian parents, there are still those times that discouragement sets in. Perhaps the following prayer should become our model and philosophy to follow in the parenting of our children:

Oh, God, Make Me a Better Parent

Help me to understand my children, to listen patiently to what they have to say and to answer all their questions kindly. Keep me from interrupting them, talk back to them and contradicting them. Make me as courteous to them as I would have them be to me. Give me the courage to confess my sins against my children and to ask of them forgiveness, when I know that I have done them wrong.

May I not vainly hurt the feeling of my children. Forbid that I should laugh at their mistakes or resort to shame and ridicule as punishment. Let me not tempt a child to lie and steal. So guide me hour by hour that I may demonstrate by all I say and do that honestly produces happiness.

Reduce, I pray, the meaness in me. May I cease to nag; and when I am out of sorts, help me, Oh Lord, to hold my tongue.

Blind em to the little errors of my children and help me to see the good things that they do. Give me a ready word for honest praise.

Help me to treat my children as those of their own age, but let me not exact of them the judgements and conventions of adults. Allow me not to rob them of the opportunity to wait upon themselves, to think, to choose, and to make decisions.

Forbid that I should ever punish them for my selfish satisfaction. May I grant them all of their wishes that are reasonable and have the courage always to withhold a privilege which I know will do them harm.

Make me so fair and just, so considerate and companionable to my children that they will have a genuine esteem for me. Fit me to be loved and imitated by my children. With all thy gifts, Oh God, do give me calm and poise and self control.

Garry C. Myers
Co-Founder and Editor
Highlights for Children
Copyright © by Highlight for Children, Inc. Columbus, OH.
1884-1971 [50]

Is successful Christian parenting possible? Yes! *With God's help, I can succeed as a Christian parent despite the challenges today's world provides.* Greater is He that is within me than he that is in the world!

Notes

1   Dahms, William. "Authority vs. Relationship," Child Care Quarterly. 7 (4), Winter 1978, p. 3.
2   Ibid., p. 3.
3   Ziglar, Zig. "Positive Steps to Developing Positive Kids," Possibilities. Summer 1986, p. 23.
4   Ibid., p. 23.
5   Gordon, Thomas. Parent Effectiveness Training. New York: Peter H. Wyden, Inc., 1972, pp. 40-44.
6   Ibid., p. 58.
7   Ibid., pp. 109-110.
8   Ibid., p. 111.
9   Ibid., p. 113.
10 Ibid., p. 114.
11 Ibid., p.52.
12 Ibid., p. 48.
13 Ibid., pp. 52-53.
14 Ibid., pp. 15-16.
15 Ibid., p. 65.
16 Ibid., pp. 66-67.
17 Ibid., pp. 67-68.
18 Ibid., p. 115.
19 Ibid., pp. 116-117.
20 Ibid., pp. 115-116.
21 Gessell Institute, Ames and Rodell. Infant and Child in the Culture of Today. New York: Harper & Row, 1943.
Gessell Institute and Ames. The Child from Five to Ten. New York: Harper & Row, 1946.
Gessell Institute. Youth: The Years from Ten to Sixteen. New York: Harper & Row, 1956.

Gessell Institute, Ames and Rodell. Infant and Child in the Culture of Today. New York: Harper & Row, 1943.

22 Norton, R.G. Parenting. New Jersey: Prentice-Hall, Inc., 1972, p. 95.

23 Ibid., p. 141.

24 Keating, Kathleen. The Hug Therapy Book. Minneapolis: Comp Care Publishers, 1983.

25 May, Gary. Child Discipline Guidelines for Parents. National Committee for Prevention of Child Abuse, 1986, p. 4.

26 Ibid., p. 4.

27 Ibid., p. 4.

28 Ibid., p. 4.

29 Krumboltz, J.D. and H.D. Changing Children's Behavior. Englewood Cliffs: Prentice-Hall, Inc., 1972, p. 78.

30 May, p. 4.

31 Maurer, A., and Wallerstein, J. "The Bible and the Rod." Berkley: The Committee to End Violence Against the Next Generation, 1982, p. 4.

32 Funk & Wagnalls Standard Desk Dictionary. New York: Harper & Row, 1984, p. 220.

33 Valusek, John E. "People Are Not for Hitting." Unpublished; used with permission.

34 Ibid.

35 Morris, Richard. Behavior Modification with Children: A Systematic Guide. Cambridge: Winthrop Pub., Inc., 1976, p. 45.

36 Dobson, James. Dare to Discipline. Wheaton: Tyndale House, 1976, p. 69.

37 Blackwood, R. Operant Control of Behavior. Akron: Exordum Press, 1971, p. 13.

38 Lerman, Saf. Parent Awareness Training: New York: A. & W. Publishers, Inc., pp. 222-225.

39 Cooperation "An Editorial without Words" Kansas City: Nazarene Publishing House.

40 Osborne, Julia. "How to Talk to Your Teenager," The Columbus Dispatch. October 4, 1987, Section C, p. 1. (used with permission)

41 McKee, Michael. Questions and Answers About Teenagers. Columbus: Ohio Psychology Publishing Co., 1984, p. 3.

42 Crystal Cathedral Ministries. "How to Talk to Your Teen — How to Talk to Your Parents," Possibilities. Garden Grove: Robert Schuller Ministries, Jan.— Feb., 1987, p. 8.

43 Gerlock, Peter. Stepfamily Association of Illinois, Inc. National Association of Homes for Children Conference, 1987.

44 Wallerstein, J. "Psychological Tasks for Children of Divorce," American Journal of OrthoPsychiatry. 53, 2, April, 1983, p. 235.

45 Gerlock.

46 Gerlock.

47 Hendricks, Howard (Ed.). Stepparents p. 409. The Encyclopedia of Christian Parenting. Old Tappan: Fleming H. Revel Company, 1982.

48 Bohannon, Paul, and Erickson, Rosemary. "Stepping In," Psychology Today. February 1978, p. 56.

49 Hendricks, Adoption p. 29.

50 Meyers, Gary. "A Parent's Prayer," Highlights for Children, Inc., Columbus, OH.

References

Blackwood, R. Operant Control of Behavior. Akron: Exordum Press, 1971, 13.

Bohannan, Paul, and Erikson, Rosemary. "Stepping In." Psychology Today, 1978, 53-59.

Channing L. What Every Family Should Know About Getting Along at Home. South Deerfield: Channing L. Bete Co., Inc. 1985, 1-15.

Crystal Cathedral Ministries. "How to Talk to Your Teen — How to Talk to Your Parents." Possibilities. Garden Grove: Robert Schuller Ministries, Jan-Feb., 1987.

Dahms, William. "Authority vs. Relationship." Child Care Quarterly. 7 (4), Winter 1978, 3-9.

Dobson, James. Dare to Discipline. Wheaton: Tyndale House Pub., 1976.

England, Robert. "Foster Care System Under Siege." Insight, 1988, 22-23.

Gerlock, P.K. National Association of Homes for Children Conference, Stepfamily Association of Illinois, Inc., 1987.

Gessell Institute, Ames and Rodell. Infant and Child in the Culture of Today. New York: Harper & Row, 1943, 157.

Gessell Institute and Ames. The Child from Five to Ten. New York: Harper & Row, 1946, 157.

Gessell Institute. Youth: The Years from Ten to Sixteen.New York: Harper & Row, 1956, 157.

Gessell Institute, Ames and Rodell. Infant and Child in the Culture of Today. New York: Harper & Row, 1943, 157.

Gordon, Thomas. Parent Effectiveness Training. New York: David McKay Co., Inc. 1970.

Hamilton, James D. Harmony in the Home. Kansas City: Beacon Hill Press of Kansas City, 1977, 91.

Hatfield, J.S., Ferguson, L.R., and Alpert, R. "Mother-Child Interaction and the Socialization Process." Child Development, 1967, 38, 365-414.

Hendricks, Howard (Ed.). The Encyclopedia of Christian Parenting. Old Tappan: Fleming H. Revell Company, 1982.

Krumboltz, J.D., and Krumboltz, H.D. Changing Children's Behavior. Englewood Cliffs: Prentice-Hall, Inc., 1972.

Lerman, Saf. Parent Awareness Training: New York: A. & W. Publishers, Inc., 1980.

Lynn, D.B. The Father: His Role in Child Development. Monterey: Broaks/Cole, 1974.

Maurer, A., and Wallerstein, J. "The Bible and the Rod." The Committee to End Violence Against the Next Generation. Berkley: The Committee to End Violence Against the Next Generation, 1982.

May, Gary. Child Discipline Guidelines for Parents. National Committee for Prevention of Child Abuse, 1986, 4.

McAdam, Elizabeth W. No Such Thing. Cleveland: Tri-Arts Lithograph Company, Inc., 1966, 9.

McKee, Michael. Questions and Answers About Teenagers. Columbus: Ohio Psychology Publishing Co., 1984.

Morris, Richard. Behavior Modification with Children: A Systematic Guide. Cambridge: Winthrop Pub., Inc., 1976, 45.

Mullins, Thomas J. When 2 or 3 Are Gathered Together Someone Spills his Milk. Waco: Word Books, 1973.

Myers, Gary. "A Parent's Prayer," Highlights for Children, Inc., Columbus, OH.

Narramore, B. Parenting with Love and Limits. Grand Rapids: The Zondervan Corporation, 1979, 118.

Newman, P., and Newman, B. Development and Its Contexts. New York: John Wiley & Sons, Inc., 1978, 185-193.

Norton, R.G. Parenting. New Jersey: Prentice-Hall, Inc., 1977, 95.

Nazarene Publishing House. Church of the Nazarene Manual. (803) 1978, 278-9.

Osborne, Julia. "How to Talk to Your Teenager." The Columbus Dispatch. Accent Section C, Oct. 4, 1987, 1. (used with permission)

Pettijohn, P., and Pettijohn, L. "Jesus Christ — Lord of the Family." Positive Parenting. Kansas City: Beacon Hill Press of Kansas City, 1983, 7.

Powell, John. Unconditional Love. Niles: Argus Communications., 1978, 76.

Schaefer, E.S. "A Circumplex Model for Maternal Behavior." Journal of Abnormal and Social Psychology, 1959, 59, 226-335.

References

Smalley, Gary. If Only He Knew. Grand Rapids: Zondervan Publishing House, 1979, 30-32.

Valusek, John E. "People Are Not for Hitting." A New Ethic (unpublished), Wichita, Kansas. (used with permission).

Wallerstein, J. "Psychological Tasks for Children of Divorce." American Journal Of OrthoPsychiatry, 53, 2, April, 1983, 230-243.

Ziglar, Z. "Positive Steps to Developing Positive Kids." Possibilities. Summer, 1986, 23.